The Dictionary of Playground Slang

The Dictionary of Playground Slang

and

A Compendium of Playground Games

edited by

Chris Lewis

First published in Great Britain in 2003 by
Allison & Busby Limited
Bon Marche Centre
241– 251 Ferndale Road
London SW9 8BJ
http://www.allisonandbusby.com

A catalogue record for this book is available from
the British Library.

ISBN 0 7490 0607 2

Printed and bound by Creative Print & Design,
Ebbw Vale, Wales

Introduction

Ever wondered what a squealing munter was? Ever been called a swamp donkey and wondered if you were being insulted? Well these and many other totally pointless queries are answered somewhere in this book.

Apart from holding the key to such trivia, the *Dictionary of Playground Slang* also contains many interesting snippets from day to day life on the school playground. There are the rules for games ranging from the slightly tame marbles, to the psychopathic aggression of maim ball. In addition there are the lyrics to some of the strange little songs we used to sing whilst skipping, hand clapping and the like. Inside you'll also find reminiscences of life as she was lived back then.

The origins of the book lie in a website I created for fun a few years ago. It started off with a nucleus of words that have been added to, corrected, and expanded by the millions of visitors the site receives. The site, known oddly enough as the Online Dictionary of Playground Slang or ODPS for short, can be found at *http://www.odps.org*. We are always looking for contributions no matter how personal, bizarre, rude or downright mucky they may be, so if reading this printed version stimulates your memory please send in any-thing you dredge up from the vaults. And don't forget to nag your family and friends into sending some in as well!

There are problems associated with editing this sort of book, of course. One of the worst is the effect it has on your every-day use of language. For example, David Shelley from Allison & Busby sent an e-mail to me saying 'Chris, you're a cult' but it was only on the third reading I realised he'd actually sent a compliment!

Please buy thls book. Maybe because you like it, or maybe because it makes the perfect gift for a prudish old aunt who is leaving her fortune to a home for geriatric cats. Or more especially buy it for me, so that I can continue to spend several hours each week hunched over a computer collecting linguistic ephemera and giggling maniacally.

By the way, the subject matter being what it is, much of the site, and therefore this book, could be considered by prudes to be a little obscene and unsuitable to be read even by the children who used the words! It's a strange old world.

Chris Lewis

A

aberdeen on a flag day (like...), adj.
quiet, peaceful. *f*. A 'flag day' is a public charity collection day where people exchange cash for lapel badges, or flags. The Scots are stereotypically stingy with money so are presumed to rather stay indoors when there is a chance they may have to part with some. Hence the streets are empty and quiet. **UK (Scot)**

ace, adj.
wonderful, first class, 'cool', really good, prob. number one. *(Ed: now forever linked to the classic TV series Red Dwarf when the character Lister, after being asked by Rimmer to call him 'Ace', said 'Ace-hole more like!')* **UK (SE)**

ace, abb.
A. C.rap E.ffort. Used to alienate kids who said 'ace'. People who originally used 'ace' to mean 'good' suddenly found that the word had been redefined to mean 'crap'. This was used in my part of Sheffield, South Yorkshire during the very early 90s and resulted in the total removal of the word 'ace' from the school vocabulary because everyone was confused as to the meaning *Circa* 1990s **UK (NE)**

acker, n.
(1) Friend;

(2) A person with no style or class;
(3) Someone from the local council estate (hard to believe kids were/are such snobs!)

Used in Basingstoke (home of ackers) but may have been invented by the contributor and his sister. Through moving away from home now believed to have spread to London and the North East. Recently more commonly used to describe anyone seen spitting/puking in the street, picking things out of bins or anyone exhibiting general proletariat behaviour.

The term originated in Somerset, England where it denotes a 'friend' or 'mate' which is where the late great entertainer 'Acker Bilk' got his name from! *Circa* 1980s (and earlier) **UK (SW)**

acrobrat, adj.
kids who attach poles to the front axle of their bikes so they can bounce up and down on the front wheel – a bit like a pogo stick on wheels. **UK**

aeroplane blonde, n.
girl with bleached/blonde hair but who still has a 'black box' **AUS**

ag, v.
abbr. of 'aggravate'. When someone was irritating, you would say 'S/He really ags me up'. Developed into a general expression of derision to be shouted at someone having any sort of bad time especially if you disliked them but weren't scared of them. Hence, if someone fell off the climbing frame head first on to the tarmac, the correct response was 'Haha! Ag!' **UK**

'ah'mer! i'm telling on you...', ph.

Sheer terror could be instilled into anyone in the contributor's school by one simple shout-aloud sentence: 'Ah'mer! I'm telling on you!' If you borrowed a girl's pencil sharpener, and it broke in contact with the merest pressure of hand, (probably because it was made in Taiwan) aforementioned young girl would wander off to teacher after saying that immortal line.

This was the mid-80s, the arse-end of the capital punishment era, which meant your bot was slapped and you were made to stand with your back to the class until dinner *Circa* 1985–91 **UK (E)**

air biscuit, n.

(1) the 'aromatic' result of breaking wind.
(2) floating poo (hi-fat crap) **UK**

air (...space), n.

The gap between the tyres and the ground when both wheels are in the air (having one tyre on the ground doesn't count). You 'catch air (space)' when you jump **UK**

al'arse/aul'arse/auldarse/allarse, adj.

pronounced 'aal-arse'. A contemptible individual, particularly one who refuses to co-operate, e.g "Ee was bein' an al'arse." *f.* prob. from 'old arse' *Circa* 1970-80s **UK (NW)**

'all-ee, all-ee, all in free', ph.

in tag or hide and seek, the phrase 'all-ee, all-ee, all in free' calls all the players back to base/home for another round of the game. Perhaps 'all-ee' is a corruption of 'all ye'; or perhaps 'ee' is just a scream modulation of 'all' to make it carry across the playground *c.f.* ollie, oxen free *Circa* 1980s **UK**

anal amigo, n.
homosexual, similar to 'bum chum' but with a 'latin' feel.
UK

analingus, v.
placing ones face into the butt cheeks of another and orally stimulating the anus with the tongue. **USA**

anchor(s), n.
brothers, sisters or any other small kids that keep you from getting out with your mates. **AUS**

ankle biters, n.
small kids *c.f.* rugrats **AUS**

ants in the pants, ph.
to squirm when seated as if one was being tickled. Rather than 'ants' these people often suffered from worms, fleas, cooties or whatever. The treatment for the condition was not to associate with them, point fingers at them and yell insults whenever possible. **UK**

antwacky, adj.
unstylish, unfashionable, old-fashioned. Possibly worn by meffers or povvos. e.g. 'Dem kecks are dead antwacky!', Contributor thinks this was in use before his era as his mother used to use it *c.f.* kecks, meffer, povvo. *Circa* 1970-80s
UK (NW)

anything man, n.
name adopted by twats when playing 'superheroes' in the playground. Most kids would be an officially licensed character from film, TV or comics (Superman, Spider-man etc.) Unfortunately, there was always one wanker who chose to be ANYTHING MAN. This would give the kid access to any

super power he wanted and at will, thus rendering the game redundant before it began. It's also interesting to note that when someone declared he wanted to be Batman, there was always some clever git who would launch into some diatribe about how Batman didn't have any actual superpowers, and if anything was more like a detective than a true superhero *Circa* 1980s **UK (Mid)**

apeshit, n.
to go apeshit means to go 'mad' or to get angry. Common usage in East Anglia, UK, but pretty universal.

apple catchers, adj.
derogatory term for someone wearing unflattering big underwear. Example: 'that fat old trout had a pair of frilly apple catchers on'. This is a term used in Herefordshire (West Country) and probably comes from this area having a large number of orchards for cider making. Contributor says it must be an old term as his dad and his mates use it and the kids in school and continue the tradition to this day. **UK (W)**

assmuncher, adj.
insulting term for someone you dislike; suggesting they are homosexual *Circa* 2002 **USA**

astronaut, n.
anus. Many words of this sort are hybrids containing a word felt to be 'obscene' but linked closely to another such that the obscene word, whilst spoken, is not undermining the inhibitions against use of 'obscene' language *Circa* 1990s
USA

ardilez, arley, arlez
meaningless expression. Corruption of ARDILES, Ozzie (footballer) **UK (SE)**

arris, n.
buttock cleft *f.* the literal meaning 'sharp edge at the meeting of two surfaces'. Strangely the term is still used with its correct meaning in bricklaying! Or possibly from 'double' Cockney rhyming slang – Aristotle=bottle, bottle and glass=arse. The latter also helps explain the term for someone who has panicked, i.e. 'lost his bottle' as in 'shit himself'.
(Ed: however, on balance I think perhaps the first is by far the most likely)

arse, n.
encompasses the whole region of the buttocks including the hole region *c.f.* arris.

arse-about-face, n.
back to front, wrong way round **UK**

'arsehole like a clown's pocket/like a wizard's cuff', ph.
used in relation to homosexuality to suggest one's anus has become excessively enlarged through overindulgence in anal intrusion.

arsehole/asshole, n.
the anus. *f.* prob. derived as contraction of 'arris hole' *c.f.* arris **UK (NW), USA**

arsehole song, rh.
first word of childhood rhyme that made 'clever' use of bad language, e.g.

> Arsehole, arsehole, a soldier I shall be
> Fuck you, fuck you for curiosity
> I'll fight for the cunt, I'll fight for the cunt
> I'll fight for the country

To piss, to piss, two pistols on my knee
Rule Britannia, two monkeys on a stick
one fell down and he landed on his
prickles grow on bushes, prickles grow on trees,
prickles grow on young girls legs just above the
knees up mister Brown one day he went to town
he took a girl behind a bush and pulled her knickers
down in Alabama…

… it goes on forever I think.

Another contributor adds the following:

Two Irishmen, two Irishmen were digging a ditch
One called the other one a dirty son of a...
Beaver, a beaver, sitting on a rock
Along came a bumblebee and stung him on his...
Cocktail, ginger ale, five cents a glass...
If you don't like it, shove it up your...
Ask me no questions, tell me no lies
Bring on the dog turds and we'll make some pies.
Rule Britannia etc...

From West London comes a third version, which is similar, yet different enough:

Mary had a little lamb, she thought it rather silly;
She threw it up into the air and caught it by its
Willy was a watchdog sitting in the grass
Along came a rattlesnake and bit him up the
Ask no questions tell no lies
Have you seen the Chinamen doing up their
Flies are a nuisance, fleas are worse
And that is the end of my silly little verse.

... and there is even a version from South Africa (*Circa* 1955):

> Ask your mother for sixpence
> to see the new giraffe
> With pimples on his nose
> and pimples on his arse.

Or, of course, there's this...

> My mother had a baby, she called him Tiny Tim,
> She took him to the lavatory to see if he could swim,
> He swam to the bottom, he swam to the top,
> When he swam to the surface she grabbed him by the cock-
> Tails, shandies, two and six a glass,
> If you don't like them, I'll shove them up your
> Ask no questions tell no lies, I saw a policeman doing up his,
> Flies are a nuisance, bees are even worse,
> I saw a doctor lying on a nurse... etc.

c.f. Rule Britannia and many others *Circa* 1950s+
UK

arse-over-head (...over-elbow, ...over-tit), v.
tripping, going head over heels, falling in an embarrassing way. *c.f.* ass-over-tea-kettle. **UK**

arsenuts, n.
lumps of solid faecal and other matter that accumulate in the hairs around the anus and between the cleft of the buttocks *c.f.* winnets, dags, cleggs. **UK (SE)**

arseways, adj.
Describes a thing held back to front or upside down e.g.

'You're holding it arseways' **UK**

'ask me bollux, ask me arse!', ph.
Term used to blow someone off, or ignore them *c.f.* talk to the hand **UK**

ass-over-tea-kettle, v.
tripping, going head over heels, falling downhill *c.f.* arse-over-head **CAN**

ass-wipe, adj.
Generally a description for a person whose intelligence would qualify him/her for little more than use as a cleanser for one's anus **USA**

aussie kiss, v.
Oral sex. Similar in the actions to a French kiss, but given 'down under' **AUS**

auntie nora, n.
The special nurse the council sent round school to check for infestations of head lice. Hence Auntie Nora the Nit Explorer *c.f.* Nitty Nora *Circa* 1980s **UK (NE)**

axe-wound, adj.
Female genitalia.**UK**

B

ba'bag, n.
scrotum, (pronounced, baw – [as in thaw]– bag) used as 'Ya
fuckin' ba' bag!' *f*. prob. abbreviation of 'ball bag'.**UK (Scot)**

baby ('Your biby 'as fell dahn the plug'ole'), poem

Heard this in my childhood and it's stuck ever since. Brilliant
stuff if very sad. No attribution however. Seems to be by
'anonymous'.

*(Ed: it was written using Cockney dialect, and this is the way it
should be read. Please use a real Cockney accent and avoid the exe-
crable version attempted by Dick van Dyke in Mary Poppins!)*

Dahn the Plug 'Ole

A muvver was barfin 'er biby one night,
The youngest of ten and a tiny young mite,
The muvver was poor and the biby was thin,
Only a skelington covered in skin;

The muvver turned rahnd for the soap off the rack,
She was but a moment, but when she turned back,
The biby was gorn; and in anguish she cried,
Oh, where is my biby?' – and the angels replied:
Your biby 'as fell dahn the plug-'ole,

Your biby 'as gorn dahn the plug;
The poor little thing was so skinny and thin
'E oughter been barfed in a jug;

Your biby is perfeckly 'appy,
E won't need a barf any more,
Your biby 'as fell dahn the plug 'ole
Not lorst… but gorn before!

UK

backer/ backy, n.

used for a lift on the back of a bike (sitting on the carrier with one leg dangling each side of the wheels). Usually in the sense of 'Giz a backer, mister!' [transl. 'Give me a lift on the back of your bike'.] **EIRE**

backshot, v.

anal sex with a female. Used as 'Did she let you backshot her?' or 'I gave her a backshot and she squealed like a pig all through it!' *Circa* 1982–87 **UK (Mid)**

bacon sarnie, adj.

police car. So called because of white/red/white colouring. Often used in conjunction with the term 'rasher' for policeman (from other slang terms for the police. i.e. 'rozzer' and 'pig'). Used as 'Look. Two rashers in a bacon sarnie!' *Circa* 1980s **UK (SE)**

bacon strip, n.

the skid-mark of faecal matter inside the underpants *Circa* 1980s **UK**

badger, n.

there's a kind of sweet called Everton Mints which are striped. In the contributor's school the sweets became a form of currency. A badger was an Everton Mint, a 'half badger' was a Trebor Mint. A 'three quarter badger' was a Trebor Refresher so someone would see whatever sweet, like an Everton Mint and say, 'give us a badger, man?' **UK (Mid)**

badger's arse, adj.
Normal use, 'As rough as a badger's arse'. Used to describe a particularly bad personal state, either due to hangover e.g. 'I feel as rough as a badger's arse' or to describe a none-too-attractive member of the opposite sex *Circa* 1990s **UK**

badger gassing, v.
to break wind in a particularly malodorous fashion **UK (Wal)**

badly packed kebab, n.
female genitalia. **UK**

bad-mouthing, v.
talk insultingly about a person or thing.
USA

bag of spanners (a face like a...), adj.
None-too-flattering description of facial features *Circa* 1970s **UK**

bagel bumper, n.
female homosexual, i.e. bagel being the bread roll with the hole, bearing some (albeit very little) resemblance to a vagina. Contributor isn't sure if the word dates to school days, and was more likely at sixth form college *Circa* 1991 **UK (SE)**

bagpuss, n.
wonderful old TV series:

Emily's cat Bagpuss
The most Important
The most Beautiful
The most Magical
Saggy old cloth cat in the whole wide world

You can find lots of detail at
http://www.smallfilms.co.uk/bagpuss/intro.htm
Circa 1980s **UK**

bag (old…), n.

unattractive female (usu.) of advancing years, uncertain temperament and dubious odour. **UK**

bags/bagsey, v.

to lay claim to a thing. Used as 'That's my seat I bagsed it just now!', 'I bagsey that horse!', 'Bags I that cake!' *Circa* 1960s – onwards **UK**

baldy slap, n.

sharp smack about the back of the head, administered to victim 'to bring good luck' in the aftermath of a haircut *c.f.* batts **UK (NE)**

balls, n.

testicles. e.g. 'I'm going to kick you in the balls,' and 'He's got huge balls!'

(Ed: always puts me in mind of this old rugby song:

> *He had large balls, large balls,*
> *Balls as heavy as lead.*
> *With a flick and a twist of his muscular wrist*
> *He'd fling them around his head… etc)*

c.f. goolies, junk, marbles, meat and two veg **Inter.**

bamp, n./adj.
scruffy, tramplike or generally unloveable person. Often used as rejoinder to one who has farted. On the other hand, to become the 'Bamp Overlord' is the ultimate rank *c.f.* ramp *Circa* 1980s **UK (NE)**

bampot, n.
Mentally ambiguous. A Scots word. Calling someone a bampot is casting aspersions on their mental faculties. Contributor doesn't know what the link is or what a bampot really is but he got called it many times as a child.
(Ed: I think this is the Scots equivalent of a chamber pot.)
UK (Scot)

banners, exc.
the word 'banners' was used in conjunction with a hand movement where your index finger was held loosely and then flicked hard onto your middle finger (pressed against your thumb) so that it made a clicking noise. Anyway, Banners was a sort of exclamation of bad luck; 'banners man' were a common pair of words together! *Circa* 1980s **UK (SE)**

bank, v.
to hit or strike with fist e.g. 'Do that once more and I'll bank ya!'.**USA**

bangers, n.
explosive fireworks. Originally a relatively harmless stick of gunpowder packed into tightly wound brown paper wrapper with a short fuse that when lit exploded with a loud noise. Banned in the UK (and most other civilised countries) when small boys discovered the dreadful things one could do with a little inventiveness – e.g. sticking them up a cat's

rectum and lighting the fuse. *f.* the noise they make when they explode *c.f.* jacky-jumper
(Ed: John tells me they are still available everywhere – why was I not informed?) **UK**

bangin', adj.

extremely desirable, used to describe a 'good thing'. Normally attached to character or physical appearance e.g. 'She's really bangin'!'**USA**

'bang like a shithouse door', ph.

insult (or invitation?) normally used in respect of a sexually liberated female who makes her own decisions about her body and who has sexual access to it – and has decided it's open to all comers *c.f.* saddle bag **UK**

barf, v.

to vomit, indulge in reverse peristalsis. OK, throwing up. It describes the action of throwing up and the stuff you throw up (i.e. puke). 'I think I'm gonna barf.' 'Well don't get barf on the floor, my parents will get mad!'

A pretty common word in elementary school and used from kindergarten up to about fourth or fifth grade *Circa* 1980s onwards **USA**

bare, ad.

substitute word for 'very', or 'lots of'. Used as 'That home-work was bare hard' and 'Ever since I took up that Saturday job, I've got bare money!' *Circa* 1980s **UK**

bargies, n.

gave 'immunity' in some games e.g. crossing the fingers when playing tag and shouting 'can't get me I've got bargies' *c.f.* barley's, fainites barley, pax etc.**UK (SW)**

barking spider, n.
rather than take blame for loud anal emissions, this provides something to blame when breaking wind loudly. Note: The name Barking Spiders was used by famed Australian rock band Cold Chisel for an incognito show at the Hordan Pavilion during the early 1970s. A live album was then released aptly titled 'The Barking Spiders Live' *Circa* current **AUS**

barley's, n.
crossed fingers when playing tick, tag etc. e.g. 'you can't get me I'm on Barley's'. Derivation possibly from the French 'parlez'. Lots of words with French origin with mangled pronunciation and meaning were introduced to the 'common' language when soldiers from Word War One returned home after spending years mingling with the French population *c.f.* bargies, vainites, pax **UK (SE)**

barney, n.
a fight. Also a shout when a fight starts e.g. 'There's a right barney going on at the back of the gym!' *Circa* 1980s
UK (NE)

barney cut, n.
a haircut resembling that of Bernard Sumner, lead singer of the group New Order *c.f.* spaz cut *Circa* 1984 **UK (NW)**

barry, n.
(1) Edinburgh slang for 'good'; 'great'; 'fantastic', as in 'That film was real barry!' Can also be seen in abundance in Irivine Welsh's book – *Trainspotting*.
(2) Embarrassing e.g. 'That was so barry'.
(3) Some weak guy who thinks he's 'well hard'. Normally seen wearing puffa jacket and jeans. Walks stupidly and smokes. **UK (Scot), UK**

bars/barsies, n.

truce word and crossed fingers as in barleys, fainites etc.
UK (S)

bashi, adj.

pronounced baa-shee. Derives from 'bad shit'. Used by garage clubbers to indicate when something is excellent...e.g. 'man dat was bashi!'**UK**

basket case, n.

it means you were considered to be insane. In 'the old days' before chemical straightjackets, the most difficult of mentally ill patients were controlled by strapping them literally into baskets. Therefore to be a basket case was to be uncontrollably mad – or more likely seriously odd or weird *Circa* 1950s+ **UK (Wal)**

batts, n.

excessive slapping about the head and ears, administered after a haircut, till the victim shouts: 'Nee (or nay) Batts!'
UK (NE)

baw-heid/baw-face, n.

used to describe a person with a large round head. e.g. 'He has a big baw face'.*f*. Scots pronunciation of BALL + HEAD, BALL + FACE. The phrase has been in common usage in the West of Scotland for decades – at least since the 50s/60s and is still in use **UK (Scot)**

baws, n.

testicles, i.e. 'balls. Used as 'Don't talk baws', 'Och yer baws', 'Your baws are rancid!' or simply as 'Baws!' *Circa* current
UK (Scot)

beacon, adj.

a person who has a large behind or more ample frame than required. Used as 'You beacon' or 'Lose some weight you beacon!' *f.* Joey Deacon (?) **UK**

beam, v.

beaming describes a girl's erect nipples e.g. 'Mary was really beaming when she did her talent show routine!' *c.f.* head-lights, high beam, peanut smuggler **USA (NE)**

beano, n.

act of torture carried out by (1) pushing thumb between first and second fingers then 'screwing' (2) rubbing someone's scalp vigorously with a clenched fist *c.f.* hundred *Circa* 1980-84

beans, rh.

classic playground rhyme. Still in current use as evidenced by Bart Simpson a few years back:

> Beans, beans the musical fruit
> The more you eat, the more you toot!
> Beans, beans they are good for your heart.
> The more you eat, the more you fart.
> The more you fart, the more you eat,
> The more you sit on the toilet seat!

bean flicker, n.

lesbian *f.* reference to masturbation of a female by stimulation of clitoris **UK (SE)**

bearded clam, n.

woman's genital area especially clitoris **USA**

beast, n.
ugly or unattractive girl *c.f.* swamp donkey **UK (SE)**

beat, adj.
incredibly ugly woman e.g. 'That chick was BEAT!' Possibly a shortened phrase 'looks like she was beaten with the ugly stick', or perhaps she simply looked like a boxer! **UK**

beat the meat, v.
male masturbation. Also called whacking off
(Ed: And any one of hundreds of other words in here) **USA**

beats, n.
A rather painful treatment that involved a whack on the upper arm for any reason imaginable *c.f.* slogs *Circa* 1984-89 **UK (Mid)**

beaver, n.
(1) large amphibious broad-tailed furry rodent of the North Americas
(2) occasionally large, nearly always furry, sometimes wet, always attached to a woman, also referred to as the pussy, snatch or even quim. Makes phrases such as 'I got attacked by a Beaver in the woods' a million times funnier. Other words include pussy and snatch *c.f.* quim. **USA**

beaver leaver, adj.
homosexual **USA**

beef curtains, n.
labia – especially when aroused. Used particularly during menstruation when the 'curtains' may be thought to resemble a raw bloody steak… *c.f.* fanny flaps **UK**

bee stings, adj.
unusually small breasts **USA**

beetle crushers, n.
large black 'Doc Marten' style boots much favoured by skin-heads. Apparently they were particularly good for crushing beetles though this would probably be achieved just as successfully with bare feet *Circa* 1985+ **UK**

beer coat, n.
the warm covering you think you have around you whilst walking home after a piss-up shortly before collapsing from hypothermia. **UK**

beer compass, n.
the internal system that gets you home after a night boozing even when you have no idea where you live, where you've been or sometimes even who you are! **UK**

beer monkeys, n.
little bastards who somehow beat you up and steal all your money while you're out drinking. You never see them, and you only learn that they have visited when you wake the next morning, feeling bruised and impoverished. Note: they should not be confused with symptoms of a bad hangover. Used as in 'Jesus H. Christ the beer monkeys got me last night!' **UK**

beer scooter, n.
invisible transport that gets you home alive after a heavy session on the pop even though you had no idea how you got there. Used as 'How the hell did I get home last night? I was smashed – I suppose I must have caught a beer scooter' **UK**

bejezus/bejesus, n.
maximise effort put into a task *f.* originated in Ireland as the oath 'by jesus', but was corrupted slightly. Was used in the film *Mad Max*.

Also an indeterminate substance mothers threatened to remove from your body when you were in the shite for some minor transgression, i.e. 'You little booger… when I catch you I'll knock the bejesus out of you! **AUS, EIRE**

bell-end, n.
insulting term (usu.) used between males. Intended to say they look like the 'glands' of a penis. Nothing sounded better at the age of 12 than calling the smelly kid in class a 'bell-end'. **UK**

bella swella, n.
jokingly offensive, similar to dick-head, bell-end. Used mainly towards friends as it sounds too stupid to be *really* offensive. Often had rhymes stuck on when being silly or someone was very stupid e.g. Bella-Swella-Della-Nella, etc. *c.f.* dick-head, bell-end *Circa* late 1980s **UK (NW)**

belm, n.
expression of doubt/disbelief (pre-chinny-reckon). Usually accompanied by a speaker putting his/her tongue in the area of the bottom teeth and bottom lip/chin causing a 'bulging' effect. The longer the 'belm', the better e.g. 'beeeeeeelllllmm-mmm' in a 'spaz' kind of voice *c.f.* chinny reck-on *Circa* 1978-ish **UK (NW)**

bender, n.
(1) a homosexual
(2) a bout of drinking to excess

bendy herman, n.

insinuation that someone is stupid and homosexual (with little justification that could be used in a court of law). Used for example as 'Eeuurrgh! Steve Jackson touched my arse! BENDY HERMAN!' In other words a spasmoid or sub-mental with homosexual leanings **UK**

benny, n/adj.

(1) stupid or excessively thick person. Also said when someone does something regarded as stupid
(2) get very angry i.e. 'throw a benny'. *f.* probably derived from a none-too-bright character called Benny on UK soap *Crossroads Circa* 1970s–80s **UK**

benson, adj.

General insult. When the contributor was at school and somebody did you a favour you could easily piss them off by saying 'Cheers Benson' instead of saying 'Thanks', to imply that they were some sort of servant or slave. This was taken from the name of the butler Benson in TV show *Soap* and his own spin off show *Benson*. For example:

> 1st Kid: 'If you are going to the van, get me 10 fags'
> 2nd Kid: 'OK, no problem'
> When 2nd Kid returns and hands over the fags the 1st Kid says: 'Cheers Benson'
> 2nd Kid then says: 'You fucking cheeky cunt I'll never do anything for you again' whilst chasing the 1st kid all over the playground.

Circa mid-1980s **UK (NE)**

beppo, adj.

also 'bep'. A derogatory term indicating that the subject of the remark is, basically, a dirty vagabond, although merely having the wrong brand of trainers is enough to prompt this remark in most South Wales schools. The term reputedly derives from a tramp of that name who lived in the Cardiff area of South Wales in the early eighties. Despite reports that the poor man has long since passed away, children as far away as Newport have been heard using the insult 'ah, yer bep', and in the town of Barry (nearer Cardiff) 'Your mum shagged Beppo' is still a fairly common playground insult, even though no one that age knows who Beppo was (or, hopefully, what 'shagged' means). **UK (Wal)**

berk, n.
an idiot, someone who does something 'stupid', or just an annoying or unpleasant person. *f.* actually derived from the Cockney rhyming slang 'Berkshire Hunt' = cunt. In the words of Michael Caine, 'Not a lot of people know that!' ... even though it's now in common use all round the UK *c.f.* burke **UK (SE)**

'berty dastard (you...)', ph.
amended form of 'dirty bastard' which kids think can be used around teachers with impunity until they are sadly disabused of that notion **UK**

b.f.d., abb.
shortened form of 'big fucking deal' which allows the phrase to be used in school with no comeback from teaching staff. **UK**

b.f.e., abb.
abbreviation for 'Butt-Fuck Egypt'. Used to denote a location considered to be at a great distance. For example, 'The parking lot was full, so my car is all the way out in B.F.E.' Used and understood extensively *Circa* 1990s+ **USA (Mid)**

bible basher, n.

person who holds a deep belief in Christianity and thus feels empowered to let everyone else know about it vocally, regardless of whether they are interested or not. Also called, albeit less often, a 'god botherer' *Circa* 1970s onwards **UK**

bidgeebuckles, n.

a curse on your opponent's turn in playing marbles or conkers to ensure they'd miss when it was their turn to play. It was said while at the same time shaking one's hand as if casting a spell *Circa* 1950s **UK**

biff, v./n.

(1) ejaculate: 'Mike couldn't control it. Just as Anne opened his zip he biffed all over the place!' (this form rarely used)
(2) punch: 'He got biffed on the snitch'
(3) person afflicted with spina bifida, but used pejoratively in a fashion interchangeable with 'mong', 'spazz', 'eppy' etc., current in the Liverpool area in the 1970s and 80s *c.f.* mong, spaz, eppy, *Circa* 1970s+**(1) S.Africa, (2/3) UK**

biffa, n.

pug-ugly. From Biffo the Bear who was a main character in the *Dandy* comic, but in VIZ comic in the 1980s there was a character called Biffa Bacon. His family were all peculiarly ugly. Biffo was actually quite reasonable looking for a cartoon bear! Biffa has also been used in HM Armed Forces for many years.

Note: We've been told that in London the more common usage of biffa, now, is to describe someone who eats a lot. It draws relevance from the popular brand of dumpster made by a company called 'Biffa' **UK (NW)**

bifter, n.
cigarette *Circa* 1990+ **UK (NW)**

biggins/biggs, n.
(1) an unimportant event or object
(2) an expression of disinterest
(3) large dark patches of sweat under the arms and across the back on a light coloured shirt – as in 'Look at the biggins on that!' *f.* 'big deal' and also from *On Safari* a UK TV show presented by Christopher Biggins, referring to the times he presented the (long-forgotten by most) show in which he was in a 'pretend' jungle but would sweat like a horse, making his shirt darker in several malodorous places! **UK (SE)**

bike (town...), n.
female who boys reckon will have, or has had, sex with anyone (seldom true!) promiscuous female

billy buttons, n.
playground name for anyone who had a nervous tic, after one of the 'Unit' kids who called himself Billy Buttons and went around asking everyone to play with him at every opportunity *c.f.* unit *Circa* 1970–80s **UK (SM)**

bin, v.
when bored, a group of boys would embark on a 'binning' expedition in the playground. A victim would be selected, captured, and then forced (arse-first) into a litter bin. It would be very hard to extricate yourself from the bin as you were doubled up and your mates would wait until you had nearly heaved yourself out before pushing you back in.

There was little shame in being binned if you struggled fiercely. Your clothes suffered from contact with the contents of the bin and sometimes wasps were trapped beneath you *Circa* 1970–80 **UK (SE)**

birmo's/burmo's, adj.

flared trousers, after they were fashionable e.g. 'Ey, look at them birmos!' *Circa* 1970 – 80s.**UK (NW)**

bitch, n./v.

(1) female dog and, by extension, a spiteful, nasty woman, one who bites.

(2) complain, criticise, be negative about something **USA**

bitchin/bitchen, adj.

used to describe something exceptionally good or really hot. e.g. 'Tom's Corvette is a set of btichen wheels.' Can also be used in a negative sense, particularly when informed of bad news to which no other reply is readily available, though only generally in third party conversations.

e.g.   Jack: 'What's up with Sally?'
         Bob: 'Her grandfather died yesterday.'
         Jack: 'Bitchin.'

USA

bitchsplitter, n.

male reproductive organ, penis *f*. Used by Man Cow of *Man Cow's Morning Madhouse*, a nationally syndicated radio program, based in Chicago. **USA**

black hole bill, n.

miserable e.g. 'The weather is black hole bill today'.**UK (NE)**

blacking, n.

initiation ceremony involving the forced undressing of a boy by other boys, to allow his genitalia to be covered in boot polish **UK**

blacking/blanking out, v.

feeling of exclusion from a desired activity. Usually the 'victim' would feel he/she had been marginalized in some form or another, perhaps excluded from a breaktime game of Kingy or some such legendary game. He would approach the main aggressor, or it might be the ringleader of a clique that had turned the others against him, and ask 'Why are you blacking/blanking me out?'

This might result in a denial and ultimately a fight, or a reason, and then ultimately a fight. Unless they were girls and it was found to be a simple misunderstanding and they hugged instead.

(Ed: of course in these enlightened days, boys can be seen hugging as well – not that there's anything wrong with that…)

For a simple misunderstanding involving boys, there would have to be some violent resolution as the victim will have had to endure 'Shame' [finger snap, finger snap] from people that saw him being blacked out and someone will have to pay for that. Similar to sending someone to Coventry *Circa* 1990s **UK**

blakey, n.

Miserable, incompetent, fascist bus inspector played by Stephen Lewis in *On The Buses*, a television sitcom broadcast during the 1970s. This subsequently became a derogatory term for a teacher *Circa* 1970s **UK**

blakes, n.

half moon shaped metal reinforcement for the bottom of shoes. (Possibly a brand name?) i.e. small metal studs with sharp points for stopping heel wear. They were cool, 'cos they let you click as you walked. Schools hated 'em 'cos they chipped and scratched the floor polish.**UK**

blanked, v.

used when you had definitely won an argument and your opponent couldn't retaliate at you and thus you would cry 'Blanked!' at them *Circa* 1980s **UK (SW)**

blaw, n.

cannabis resin. e.g. 'He smokes blaw' Note: rhymes with 'floor'. *f.* Scottish pronunciation of 'blow'. Note: Cocaine is called 'blow' in the USA **UK (Scot)**

blep, n.

Epileptic. Either used literally or pejoratively *Circa* 1970-80s. **UK (NW)**

blert, n.

foolish person. Someone of limited intelligence. Still used in suburbs of Liverpool as a derogatory term, i.e. 'Eh mate... you fuckin blert?' mainly by pensioners queuing for Giros at the post office *c.f.* spaz, dickhead *Circa* 1980 onwards **UK (NW)**

blimp, n.

(1) An overweight, overbearing, over-nationalistic, over-critical person. Named after a WWII cartoon character created by David Low.
(2) A WWII balloon which floated in the sky over London during air raids to protect important defence installations from the attacks of low flying aircraft and bombs. Named for their shape after the cartoon character.
(3) Someone who is fat and can't run, but runs anyway and makes a fool of himself. Like the turtle blimp on *Ninja Turtles*. Fat Blimp... From the same source *Circa* 1930s–to date **UK**

blind, n.

unfortunate e.g. 'Your old man won't let you come to the

party? That's blind!' **S. Africa**

bling-bling, n.
ostentatious jewellery, can also be used to indicate personal wealth in general *Circa* 1990s **USA**

blob, n.
condom **UK (NE)**

'blob (on the...)', ph.
menstruation, experiencing one's period .**UK (EA)**

block, n.
head e.g. 'I'll knock your block off!'**UK (NW)**

blocky/blockie 1-2-3, n.
outdoor variation of hide and seek, where the hiders have to try and touch the 'block' (lamp-post) without getting caught by the seeker, shouting 'Blocky 1-2-3 in!'. Another variation has the chanter saying 'poddy poddy 1-2-3 in!'

bloodclot (blurclar), n.
(1) a tampon
(2) someone who is a fool, and no time should be wasted on.
(3) a person who can be used for one purpose and then disposed of.

blowing chunks, v.
vomiting **USA**

blow, v.
pass wind, fart **UK**

blow in, n.
a pest that isn't usually seen in an area but appears after a

period of heavy wind or storm. Has now become synonymous with someone new in town who buzzes around making noise and disturbing locals **AUS**

blow-job, n.
term for oral sex performed on a male.

blow pies, v.
to vomit. 'I drank so much I'm going to blow pies'
Circa 1990s **USA (Penn)**

bludger, n.
a person who is lazy or won't work, although nowadays the
word is mainly associated with the balls in Quidditch (from
the 'Harry Potter' books) *Circa* 1950s onwards **AUS, UK**

bludgeon, n.
(1) to beat, normally to death, with a heavy object (original
meaning)
(2) claim dole, or otherwise feed off society but contribute
nothing **(1)UK, (2)AUS**

blue goldfish, n.
initiation rite *f*. Newbies would be asked if they'd like to
'Come see the Blue Goldfish' then be taken into the toilets,
their head forced into the toilet pan ... and the thing flushed
and flushed, ad infinitum. Also called bogwash. **UK (Mid)**

blue vein, n.
penis *Circa* 1960s+ **AUS, UK**

BMX, n./v./abbr.
Bicycle Moto Cross. The early 1980s sport involving light,
gearless bicycles for races and stunt competitions, a bicycle

designed for this purpose *c.f.* burner, chopper etc.

bob, v./n.
to defecate e.g. 'I've bobbed my pants!', 'I've got bob on my shoes!'**UK (NE)**

bob, n.
the time a girl spends menstruating **UK**

BOBFOC, n.
acronym – Body Off *Baywatch*, Face Off *Crimewatch* **UK**

B.O. biter, adj.
someone with offensive body odour **UK**

bock/bok, n.
to break, dismantle, disassemble, trash *f.* regional dialect word used in schools around Plymouth **UK (S)**

bodacious, adj.
jolly good. Rather nice, excellent actually *Circa* 1950s–70s **USA**

boff, v./n.
(1) to have sexual intercourse with
(2) to break wind, fart etc. used in Lancashire school in early 1970s. Particularly amusing when a certain Ms Hough (aged 9) farted, when we could all cry out 'Hough's Boffed!,
(3) swot, a teacher's pet (prob. abbr. of 'boffin')
(4) word for sweets such as Mojos and Cola Bottles etc. Seller of said items would be referred to as 'The Boff Man' or 'The Boffy' **UK**

boff your ring, v.
to be sick so violently after a night out it felt like you'd

thrown up your own anus. For example, 'I drank 14 pints then boffed my ring!' *Circa* 1994–2001 **UK (Wal)**

bogs, n.

toilets... e.g. 'we were smoking in the bogs when Miss Jones busted us.'

bogging, adj./v.

(1) smelly

(2) looking at someone in an offensive manner (question is posed as a threat). e.g. 'You boggin' at me?'. The answer, usually in accusatory manner in same context, is traditionally, 'You got a problem?'

(3) Can refer to the act of excretion, used as in 'I'm going a' bogging.'

(4) Also used to represent a jag, or comedown from a narcotic (usually pot, or something else that makes you lethargic). The literal feel for the word in the area is that 'to bog' is to feel extremely weighty, or 'bogged down' and this causes you to lay about with lethargy/laziness. Basically, 'man, we're outta weed... I'm soooo boggin'... Someone should go out and get some munchies...' **(1,2,3)UK, (4)Can**

bogwash, n.

See 'blue goldfish' **UK**

BOHICA, ac.

acronym for 'Bend Over, Here It Comes Again'. Describes a situation where you feel you're being dealt with unfairly, i.e. you're being screwed *Circa* 1980s **USA**

boiler (old...), n

a sexually desperate woman of advancing years who tries to pass herself off as a teenage girl in the hope of persuading some poor pissed guy that she's worth a try. Often found hanging round clubs on 'Grab a Granny' nights **UK (Wal)**

bollocks, n./adj.
(1) the male testes.
(2) pathetic, worthless *c.f.* satchel

bollixed, n./adj.
very drunk, ruined, messed up **UK**

BOMBI, n.
acronym for 'Bottom Of My Balls Itch' *c.f.* swamp **USA**

bone of contention, n.
an erection that causes an argument e.g. one that arises when a man is watching beach volleyball on TV with his girlfriend **AUS**

bone hawg/bone hog, n.
sexually active female, a woman who enjoys performing oral sex on men **USA**

boner, n.
erection **UK**

bonk, n.
sexual intercourse *f.* A UK TV show called *TisWas* – introduced by Chris Tarrant amongst others.

The cult show, originally a children's programme, was famous for many oddball jokes and even created a 'hit' dance called, the 'Dying Fly' which pretty much revolved around people lying on the floor on their backs and waving arms and legs in the air. And who will ever forget 'The Bucket Song'?

Anyway... Bonk was reportedly created by reversing the word 'knob' and applying it as a description to women's 'naughty bits'. It quickly mutated into a euphemism for the sexual act itself. It spread over the world and has remained a favourite substitute for other better known but more offensive Anglo-Saxon terms for sexual intercourse. **UK**

bonker, n.
a type of marble that was the next size up from the regular marble and usually worth 3 or 4 marbles in equal value. But not worth quite as as much as a ball-bearing *c.f.* marbles, **UK (S)**

bonkers, adj./v.
insane. Performing crazy behaviour, to act or be bonkers is to act in a crazy or erratic manner. In current use in UK.
UK

bonza, adj.
'cool' or 'excellent'. For example, if someone manages to raid their parent's stash of booze and turn up at a party with a few bottles of booze then they might say 'bonza mate!' *Circa* 1930s+ **AUS**

boonshniggle, v.
unbelievable. **UK (Scot)**

boot (to...), v.
to indulge in reverse micturition, i.e. vomit **USA**

boost, v.
to leave, depart e.g. 'I'm knackered. I'm going to boost'
UK (Scot)

booty-cheddar, n.
bullshit, nonsense. Used as 'Quit spittin' all that booty-cheddar!' **USA (S)**

boracic/brassic, adj.
short of cash *f.* cockney rhyming slang... boracic lint=skint **UK**

botty-blasts, n.
not loud farting but a situation where a football is repeatedly vollied at someone's arse, by a lot of people **UK (NW)**

Bournville Boulevard, n.
anus, arse, bum etc., but always with homosexual connotations. Bourneville is the Birmingham village where the Cadbury's chocolate factory is. And it doesn't take a genius to work out that chocolate is the same colour as shit, hence the phrase.

Thus, 'Going up Bourneville Boulevard' is to perform anal intercourse. **UK (Mid)**

bovver-boots, n.
big boots worn by punks and hard-cases... most often Dr Martens *c.f.* beetle crushers **UK**

bowfin, adj.
'horrible' or 'really disgusting or dirty/smelly' as in 'yer socks are bowfin!'. Note: 'Bow' is pronounced as if to rhyme with 'cow' **UK (Scot)**

boy in the boat (little...), n.
clitoris *Circa* 1990s **AUS, UK**

brace-face, n.
rude name for someone wearing braces on their teeth *c.f.* tin-grin, metal mouth **USA**

brain bucket, n.
helmet for cycling, horse riding etc. **UK**

41

brainfart, n.
the cause of an effect noticeable when, for example, you are speaking and lose your train of thought. Used as 'So I went to the store and um... uh-oh brainfart... oh yeah… and bought some milk' **UK**

brassings, n.
also 'hard brassings' was said whilst rubbing the chin a la 'chinny-reckon'. It was said whenever you were mocking someone else's misfortune e.g. falling over in playground, missing an easy goal in football, clay pot blowing up in kiln in art etc *Circa* Early 1980s *c.f.* chinney reck-on, Jimmy Hill etc. **UK (Mid)**

bray, v.
to beat, hit, strike repeatedly. Usually employed in reference to a beating by someone in authority, either teacher or parent, but by extension came to include also a beating or (more often) a threatened beating from another youth. For example, 'If you don't stop being such a twat yer mum'll bray you'.

When the beating was administered by another youth the more usual term would be 'batter', as in 'I'm gonna batter you' *Circa* 1970s–90s **UK (NE)**

'break the seal', ph.
urination. Specifically the first piss of the evening after boozing steadily for hours. When you've been once to 'break the seal' you will find you will need to keep going every few minutes for the rest of the night **UK**

breville devil, n.
term denoting frenzied experimental masturbator. Certain models of Breville sandwich toasters came with special plastic tongs for removing the lethally hot toasted sandwiches from the machine (doubtless because someone had probably

in the past burnt their hands trying to do so and sued the company). Allegedly, someone used said tongs to beat himself off with. Needless to say, toasted sandwiches ceased to be a popular snack in his boarding house. Originated at the The Leys School, Cambridge **UK (SE)**

brick, v.
to shit oneself in fear especially when hard lads are chasing you down the alley: brickin' yourself

broady, n.
bike stunt which involves pulling on the back brake on your Chopper/BMX/Chipper/Grifter and swinging it round kicking up the gravel **UK**

brothel creepers, n.
popular sort of footwear with very thick flat rubber soles that allow you to walk almost silently. Very useful for creeping up behind people to give them wedgies or cop a feel. Similar to the platform soles favoured by 'Baby Spice' but worn (usu.) by males *Circa* 1940s-1960s **UK (Wal)**

brown wings, adj.
expression used between nineties males to express their prowess at drilling the marmite motorway of female sexual partners e.g. 'Have you got your brown wings yet?' Never used in describing homosexual relations. *Circa* 1990s **UK (Wal)**

bruce (to...), v.
to 'Bruce' essentially means having to leave a party or the pub when all your mates are staying to continue getting hammered. Originally derived from Bill Bixby's portrayal of 'Bruce Banner' in the 70s TV series of *The Incredible Hulk*, which always ended with a melancholy shot of Bruce walk-

ing off into the distance, doomed to wander the earth alone. Used as 'I'm going to miss my last bus, I'll have to Bruce' *Circa* 1990s **UK (S)**

bruce lee, adj.
erect nipples – as in 'hard nip' **UK**

bubble, n.
(1) notably bulbous caricature of a foreskin
(2) an excessively stupid or unpleasant person **UK (SE)**

bucklenut, adj.
basically someone who is a bit thick, slow, no common sense etc. Or if someone has done something completely stupid or is being dense and you can't think of a putdown this might come in handy *Circa* 1990s **UK (NE)**

bud, adj.
dreadful, bad. e.g. 'That is so bud' as in something that is really crap. Very big in the eighties in Swindon, *f.* bad **UK (SW)**

budget, n.
used to describe a situation, an object, a person, or a place that is rubbish/disappointing, or basically shit! For example 'This place is budget!' or 'You're so budget!' Basically a derogatory term implying the person is 'cheap rubbish', or hasn't a clue about the truth of an issue. For example if you are telling a joke and the other person doesn't understand the joke, then that person is 'budget' or if a group of friends are watching a film and one person doesn't find it funny, when everyone else does, then that person is 'budget'.
UK (SE)

budgie, n.
a make of Raleigh bike: a junior version of the chopper with the characteristic drop handle bars and way-out front/back wheel ratio of its larger counterpart *c.f.* Chopper **UK (SE)**

budgie jacket, n.
satin bomber jacket with elongated 'penny round' collar as worn by Adam Faith in his weekly ITV Soho underworld adventures in *Budgie Circa* 1971 **UK**

budgie's tongue, n.
female 'erection' **UK**

bug-fucker, n.
someone with an unusually small penis

bug rake, n.
comb e.g. 'lend us yer bug rake... ma head's itching... *f.* head lice were very common in that era *c.f.* nitty nora *Circa* 1940s **AUS**

bugs, n.
mysterious disease or ailment transmitted to you by getting to close to someone who was dirty or smelly, and that you could in turn transmit to other people by touching them e.g. if you got too close to someone who was dirty you then had 'the bugs'.

People who were particularly dirty were called either 'bugsy boy' or 'bugsy girl'. *Note:* You could protect yourself from the bugs by clutching the top of your arm (I imagine this came from holding the area where you had your inoculation jab) and shouting, '1,2,3,4,5 bugs injection all over for life'. This was a primary school practice and died out by the time you got to secondary school *c.f.* fleas-inject **UK (Scot)**

bull (milk a...), rh.

Milk a bull
Milk a bull
Only one tit and it's hard to pull

Circa 1940s–60s **UK (Wal)**

bum, n.
anus and surrounding area including buttocks. Hence the use in the USA to describe homeless people and beggars. Likewise, the term is used for someone who is useless or shiftless, like son-in-laws or football coaches. ('Ya bum!') **USA**

bum-chum, n.
male homosexual. **UK**

bum-crumbs, n.
faecal material that clings to anal hairs *c.f.* arsenuts **UK**

bumps, n.
birthday game where victim was held spread-eagled by arms and legs raised in the air and dropped such that their buttocks struck the floor with force. One bump was administered for each birthday *c.f.* pinch-punch, dumps **UK**

bundle, n.
shouted whenever a fight was taking place (or in the disco when you were feeling bored) and involved everyone 'bundling' someone, generally a younger boy. A bundle is when a group of boys leap on and force another boy to the ground. Generally involves at least three people, often leading to more and more people joining, leaping on until a large

pile of boys is formed. It is, of course, very painful (hopefully) for whoever is it at the bottom of the bundle **UK**

bung hole, n.
anus. Used on *Beavis and Butthead*, when Beavis drinks coffee he becomes corn-holio, and he says 'I need TP for my bung hole.' Bung hole is slang for butt hole *Circa* 1990s **USA**

bunking slip, n.
piece of paper to be signed by the teacher of every class on your timetable, then returned to the registration teacher the next day to prove you went to all your classes. Given to bunkers when caught bunking off school **UK (Scot)**

bunnidge, n.
used in a phrase taunted at people when they were supposed to be ashamed about something e.g. 'Feeeeel the bunnidge!' **UK (W)**

bunny-hop, n.
BMX stunt making the whole bike jump in the air. Best done by crouching over the handlebars and 'exploding' upwards. Done this way it helps you clear obstacles like logs and kerbs.**UK**

burke, n.
an idiot. *f.* local adaptation of the UK 'berk' because of 'Wills and Burke', two early Australian explorers who unfortunately got lost and died *c.f.* berk **AUS, NZ**

burn, n.
BMX stunt. A 'burn'is often described the result of riding up to your mate's bike (whilst it was also in motion) and touching his back tyre with your front tyre, resulting in a wonderful 'zipppp' noise and a friction burn mark on each tyre. Most

often used in the context, 'I'm gonna burn you up!' which usually triggered frantic pedalling and squeals as the victim tried to out-run his pursuer.

Always misunderstood by adults. Tell your dad that 'Matthew was trying to burn my tyre!' and he would storm round Matthew's house, full of misconceptions involving blow-torches and lighter fluid *Circa* late 1970s–mid-80s
UK

burner, n.
entry level Raleigh BMX bike. Basic, black painted with gold flame effects...sad 'losers bike' *Circa* 1980s *c.f.* BMX, chopper
UK

bushie, bush pig, n.
really physically unattractive – well OK, ugly – girl who can only be likened to something even grosser in appearance and habit than a domestic pig. The term Bush Pig is already quite common in Australia. The bush pig is the sort of ten-pinter you might wake up with after a really heavy night on the pop *c.f.* ten-pinter, *Circa* 1990s–current **AUS, UK**

bus stop posse, n.
generally used to refer to the teenage boys and their girl-friends, usually wearing cheap tracksuits and trainers, who hang around in bus stops drinking cans of beer, or squishy bottles of cider, because they can't get into any pubs due to their age *c.f.* kappa slappa

butter face, adj.
girl with a gorgeous body and ugly face. Used as in 'She's got a nice body – but 'er face...'

C

caffle, v.

to get caught up, entangle. e.g. when playing conkers the strings 'got all caffled up.' **UK (Wal)**

cak/cack/cacky/kak, n.

excrement e.g. 'cack face.' Also 'He got kakked on for shouting in the passage.' Variations are very common all over the world. Raises difficult questions as to whether words used from another language count as slang. *f.* direct mutated transposition from the Afrikaans 'kak' for 'shit' – which of course raises the question of the origin of the colour 'khaki'! **UK, S. Africa**

cackersarnie, n.

to describe the act of pulling someone's underwear up so high that it nearly cut them in two. Quite literally cacker (shit) sarnie (sandwich). Used amongst girls and boys but mainly boys inflicting it on other boys *c.f.* wedgie *Circa* 1980-86 **UK (SE)**

camel toe, n.

(1) when a girl's trousers are too tight and you can see the outline of her vaginal lips she is 'showing her (Camel's) hoof off'. This is because it resembles the camel's hoof that has two parts and a slit in the middle.

(2) a clitoral wedgie *Circa* 2002 **UK**

camping (to go...), n.
mincing up and down in front of a boy thought (or known) to be homosexual in order to humiliate him **UK (Wal)**

cancer foot, adj.
describes a person who has had a shot at goal, resulting in the ball swerving off five miles away from the goal **UK**

cane/caner, n.
to be 'told off' or to be badly beaten at something (not normally physically). Anything really bad, so to receive a caning is to get told off: 'He caned you!', 'You got a real caning there!' **UK**

cankle, adj.
leg (usually belonging to a female) when the calf goes directly into the foot with no definition of an ankle *c.f.* keg-legs *Circa* 1980s **UK**

carrot top, n.
a gentle term for a ginger person **UK**

cartwheels, n.
boys' game: involved encouraging or daring girls in skirts or dresses to do handstands so you could see their underwear. **UK**

casey, n.
proper leather football. Size 5 Casey's were the things to have and required someone's dad to have a funny little adapter for the bike pump. Invariably no one's dad did, and the ball would go flat. Almost always banned at schools owing to

window/head smashing capabilities *Circa* 1980–90s **UK (NE)**

catalogue shopper, adj.

used as an insult to mean your parents didn't have enough money to buy things for cash so had to buy on the 'never-never' from catalogues which didn't have the best quality gear so, even with 'new' clothes on, you always looked like a saggy, daggy twat *c.f.* yellow packet *Circa* 1980s **UK**

caterpillar, n.

the one old-skool breakdance move that even a spacker can master *c.f.* windmill

cat's prick, n.

over-elongated burning end of a cigarette that is created when a group of people pass it round and smoke it very quickly.

Imagine 5 or 6 lads in the boys' bogs passing round a Benson & Hedges. By the time it's almost finished the burning ember is about an inch long, and someone would always exclaim, 'look at the fuckin' cat's prick on that!' *Circa* 1982 **UK (SE)**

cat's whisker, n.

(1) old name for a small crystal radio. Very weak reception so needed headphones, but did (and does) work
(2) 'code' name for British Bulldog **UK**

CBS, ac.

(pronounced ceebs) Acronym for 'Can't be arsed'. When you say 'I have CBS' it means you can't be arsed with anything in particular. Contributor said it summed up his time at Chipping Campden School, and may in fact sum up many people's lives. **UK (SE)**

chad, n.

cartoon 'egg' peering over a brick wall, usually saying 'Wot no school?' or similar **UK (SE)**

chainey, n.

one person was 'it' and whoever they 'got' had to hold their hand (or if it was a member of the opposite sex you held their sleeve), and so on, until you ended up with 20 kids gripping onto each other and running round the playground **UK (SE)**

chalk (to...), v.

also known as dustpatch: to chalk someone before a class, to mark them with your mark without their knowledge, normally using a board rubber. Less used now due to white board introduction. Once done, it is brought to their attention either by slow teasing or brazenly in the presence of a staff member **UK (SE)**

charlie/charlie chester, n.

child molester (term often used for headmasters) *c.f.* rhyming slang – no specific insult intended towards the UK comedian of that name **UK (NW)**

'charlie's dead', excl.

a shout at a girl whose petticoat was showing. Origins unknown. **UK**

charver/chava/chav, adj.

'He's a right little Charva'. Used to describe group of youths usually described as 'townies' or 'kappa slappers' elsewhere. Charva's typically wear things like Kappa tracksuits and Berghaus jackets, smoke Lambert and Butler cigarettes amongst other things, have gold-hoop earrings, spit constantly and wear at least one gold sovereign ring (a gold band attached to the bottom of a gold sovereign coin) on each hand.

Most people seem to grow out of 'charvadom' by their early twenties, although may still carry a few of the habits through to later life and will by then probably drive a souped-up XR2I, with blacked-out rear windows and a 5000 watt stereo system. Another trait common to the charva is a loud, slightly sarcastic, nasal laugh and slow 'can't really be bothered to talk' speech.

Typical slang words that Charvas use are 'belta', 'mint' and 'waxa' all meaning good or great, with the prefix of 'pure' or 'total' this would mean really good (I couldn't be bothered to send separate entries for these words, sorry). The word charva has been in common use in the North East since the mid-nineties *Circa* 1990s **UK (NE)**

cheapie, adj.

derived from 'cheap thrills'. Used to denote that the activity that a schoolmate was finding pleasure in was one that the speaker did not think was up to much at all, and was, in all truth, a bit gay (to use the terms bandied about at the time).

Geeky child:	'I really like classical music'
Hard, sporty child:	'Cheapies!'

Circa 1980s **UK (NE)**

checks, n.

word used to indicate that you have just farted and are proud of it. Also used in conjunction with a hand movement: The hand movement was a 'thumbs up', lick the end of the thumb, and point the thumb down in a 'Roman' finish-him-off way. Eventually was used, without saying 'Checks' to warn your closest friend that you had 'let one go' and that you would recommend legging it immediately *c.f.* fart, legging it. **UK**

check the oil level, v.
slide a finger into a vagina *Circa* 2001 **CAN**

cheebah/chebe-ah/cheebahz, n.
small. Originated as a small plastic toy based on a character from a Japanese animated show/movie. Noted for disproportionately large heads and eyes, small bodies and no noses. Can also be used as an insult to a boy or compliment to a girl *Circa* 1990s **UK**

cheekpulls, n.
form of torture, holding down victim and pinching his/her cheeks really hard.

cheeky-sweat, n.
reprimand e.g. if someone grabbed half the bag of crisps when offered one, you would shout 'get off, yer cheeky sweat!!' *Circa* 1980-81**UK (NW)**

'cheese it!', ph.
instruction to run, or action. Its use is another form of 'leg it', meaning for everyone to run away. Expletive can be placed before phrase to indicate the urgency for departure *c.f.* leg it *Circa* 1998 **UK**

chelp/chelping, n./v.
rubbish, and talking rubbish *Circa* 1990s **UK**

cherry, n.
(1) derog. A child considered to be so stupid he must have had a brain meltdown *f.* Chernobyl disaster, in the Ukraine (former USSR).
(2) virginity

cherry picker, n.
(1) a guy who whose main aim in life is to have sex with virgins.
(2) a guy who seems to spend all day scratching his scrotum and testicles **USA**

chickenhead, n.
(1) a stupid person that wanders around aimlessly like a decapitated chicken (usually refers to women)
(2). a woman performing oral sex on a man – because her head bobs like a chicken's. Commonly used in rap or hip hop *Circa* 1999 **USA**

china, n.
(1) friend (Cockney rhyming slang, China plate=mate).
(2) marble: an opaque, mainly white, version *c.f.* alley, enner, bosher, king etc.**UK**

chinese backage, n.
telling someone to go all the way to the front of a queue (which the other people in the queue generally won't allow). 'Chinese frontage' is therefore the opposite, i.e. telling someone to go all the way to the back of the queue. **AUS**

chinese burn, n.
playground punishment/torture consisting of the rotation of skin near the wrist in two opposing directions simultaneously causing friction burns or a sensation of heat in the victim's forearm *c.f.* Japanese burn

chinese haircut torture, n.
as kids, you would get a long stalk of grass, the type with the seeds in a bunch at the top. The seeds would then be removed by gripping the stalk at the base with one hand and with the other hand sliding upwards to shed the 'flower' part

without snapping it off.

The stalk would then be twisted into the unsuspecting victim's neck hairs several times until a good grip was obtained, and then firmly yanked. This produced the desired effect of a loud scream accompanied by a bunch of neck-pubes and a very sore neck *Circa* 1960s **UK**

'ching chong chinaman', poem

another poem highlighting a play on words:

> Ching Chong Chinaman sitting on the grass,
> Along came a bumblebee and stung him on his...
> Ask no questions, tell no lies,
> I saw a policeman doing up his...
> flies are a nuisance, bugs are even worse,
> And this is the end of my silly little verse.

c.f. Arsehole Song, Johnny was a wanker, Rule Britannia *Circa* 1960s **UK**

chinny reck-on, n.

expression indicating disbelief (sometime accompanied by the phrase... 'toooo baaaaddd' *c.f.* Tutenkhamun

chipper, n.

A small Chopper bike *c.f.* chopper

choad/chode/choda, n.

(1) penis that's wider than it is long
(2) The skin located between the male reproductive organ (penis) and the arsehole. The contributor says this was the common meaning when he was a child, but he's never heard the other definition printed. This meaning of the word is found in the US predominantly, but it is also used by children

in England and other English-speaking countries. Can be used as an insult e.g. 'You choad-licker' *Circa* 1998+ **AUS**

chocha, n.
female genitalia. Used e.g. 'Shave yo chocha' or 'Put yo' face all in ma chocha!' *Circa* 2000 **USA**

chock/chocker, v.
homosexual anal intercourse. Possibly limited to only a few schools **AUS**

choccy, n.
particularly gruesome form of gob produced by consuming chocolate prior to expectorating on the victim. A contributor writes: 'A choccy produced by one friend of mine was visible on the wall of the gym for over nine months, but that was partly because mould and moss had started growing on it.' *Circa* 1970s-80s **UK (NW)**

chod, n.
(1) piece of excrement
(2) derog. term for unusually immature person who is baby-ish in their behaviour **UK (N)**

CHODA, n.
acronym for 'Cunt Hair On Da Ass'. Mostly used to describe female pubic hairs but can also be used to describe male pubic hairs as well. For example, 'Did you see that bitch's choda sticking out of her pants?' *c.f.* spider's legs. *Circa* 2000 **USA**

chokker/choc, n.
great, wonderful, magic, excellent *f.* chocolate **UK (NE)**

chomps, n.

sweets, used as 'Got any chomps?', or 'Gi'us some o' yer chomps eh?' Originally a chocolate bar with fudge inside that cost 10p. Came to be known as sweets in general *Circa* 1980s **UK (NW)**

chops, n.

talk too much, be cheeky. e.g. 'Don't chops to him, he's nails!' **UK (Wal)**

chopper, n.

model of bicycle manufactured by Raleigh during the 1970s, featuring odd-sized wheels, high handlebars, a banana saddle and possibly a fake raccoon tail on a pole as well. The Chopper line went (largest to smallest): Chopper, Chipper, Tomahawk, Budgie. **UK**

chore, v./n.

(1) to steal – 'Did you chore those sweets from the shop?'
(2) a person, usually male. Can be used in a variety of ways e.g. 'Alright chore!', 'Oi! Chore!' *Circa* 1990s **UK (NW)**

christening, n.

ceremony of having people kick the crap out of your new shoes – particularly bad if Dr Marten shoes – seen as a token of hardness. **UK (S)**

chuck a willy, v.

have a temper tantrum. Similar to 'spit the dumm', 'chuck a wing ding' etc *Circa* 1980s **AUS**

chuddy, n.

testicles. Used if you are proved correct at the expense of someone being incorrect. Can be used also as an 'I'm better than you!' comment. Usually used in the phrase: 'eat my chuddies' whilst pointing at your crotch. (Note: Chuddie is actually Gujurati for underpants). *Circa* 1990s **UK**

chuddle, n.
animal excreta, used as in 'Ewww... I just stepped in some bird chuddle' **USA**

chud nuts, n.
lumps of dried poo stuck in bum hair. *Circa* mid 1990s **UK (SE)**

chuff, n.
(1) anus, commonly used in 'Tighter than a gnat's chuff' to mean tight-fisted
(2) fart **UK**

chuffy badge (do you want a ...), n.
derisive comment to make to someone who has been showing off **UK**

chunder, n.
vomit *f.* term from cruise voyages, a contraction of 'watch under' *c.f.* spew **AUS**

clacker, n.
the anus or rectum – probably from cloaca. **UK**
clacker (stuff it up your...), n.
exclamation intended signifying forceful rejection of an idea or point of view. **UK**

clacker valve, n.
female genitalia *Circa* 1990s **UK**

claggy, adj.
smeared with, or covered in excreta... e.g. 'Oh geez... I trod in

dog chocolate, now my shoes are all claggy!'

clag nut, n.

the bits of loose toilet paper stuck to your bum after taking a dump **UK**

clamped, adj.

used in an argument, when one party has argued with such skill or volume that the other person is unable to respond. That first party would then announce to the other party that are clamped with an exclamation such as: 'That's YOU clamped, mate,' or: 'Kerrr-LAMPED!' Used in the Hull area in the mid to late eighties. Often used to silence the second party even when first party may not have necessarily won the argument, as the declaration of 'clamped'-ness would often cause any observers to also shout it at the second party, thus drowning out any possible protests against ill-followed paths of logic. In this way, 'clamped' was often an easy way out of an argument, especially if you were playing to a crowd *Circa* 1980s **UK**

clanking (...for it), v.

'quaint' saying from a secondary school, i.e. 'The bitch was clanking for it' meaning a young lady was aroused and wanted sex. Usually a complete lie and said in the company of your male mates when asked to talk about your date with 'X' the previous night *Circa* 1973-79 **UK (SE)**

clatty, adj.

exceptionally dirty, the most disgusting level of dirt imaginable. Usually refered to an item. e.g. 'that's pure clatty', or a person e.g. 'By Christ, he's a clatty bastard' **UK (Scot)**

clay class, n.

thick, stupid, mentally insecure. Named for Special Needs

pupils forced to make objects out of clay during 'all-day art sessions'. Hence derogatory term 'he's in the clay class' meaning 'he's a thick twat', or 'Jesus, you oughta be in the clay class' *Circa* 1990s **UK (Wal)**

cleg, n.
used in the north of Ireland to denote a species of parasitic fly of the sort that chases you and bites into your skin in boglands and some country areas. Therefore a 'cleg' is someone who in other words is a leech or a parasite, or a generally obnoxious person. Used as in 'He's a fucking cleg' *Circa* 1990s **UK (NI)**

cleggs, n.
lumps of solid faecal and other matter that accumulate in the hairs around the anus and between the cleft of the buttocks *c.f.* arsenuts, dags, klingon **UK (NE)**

clip a steamer, v.
defecate *c.f.* drop the kids off, release the hounds. **USA**

clogsies, n.
clogsies, along with the action of crossing index and middle fingers on both hands, indicated immunity to getting the lurgi, thus that person could not be 'on' or 'it' at that time *c.f.* injectified, lurgi *Circa* 1970s **UK**

coachman's knob, n.
erection gained on public transport. Often achieved on the school bus, a combination of vibrations through the seat and the proximity of attractive females! *Circa* 1980+ **UK (Scot)**

cobb, n./v.
a coughed up chunk of phlegm usually spat for distance and accuracy to the amusement of your pals *Circa* 2001 **CAN**

cob nut, v.

to smack somebody on the back of the head with your hand in a fist, but making contact with your fingers rather than the knuckles. e.g. 'Give him a cob-nut'. Culled from contributor's painful experience in East Anglia. **UK**

cock blocking, v.

to prevent another male moving in on your female companion with a view to alienating her from your affections.

cock of the year/school, n.

hardest (that is to say, strongest, most dangerous) member (that is to say pupil) of the year/school. Title usually achieved by a series of fights/scraps with other would-be 'hards'. Eventually one person would come out as hardest/most solid. This person would be best avoided but would probably never be seen at school anyway (owing to them skiving) *Circa* 1990+ **UK (NE)**

coffin (the...), n.

the school canteen where meals of unutterable awfulness were served on a regular basis **UK (Wal)**

'collars and cuffs don't match', ph.

suggestion that the colour of head hair and pubic hair differs. Used usually as some sort of insult towards women whose hair has been dyed blonde *Circa* 1950s+ **UK**

comb-over, adj.

style of haircut, which looks almost like a quasi-shreddie. Is used to describe both the style and the person employing it. The gentleman, who is almost bald, insists on growing the remaining hairs at the side of his head long enough to comb them over the rest of the scalp. This, they misguidedly believe, gives the illusion of having hair whereas, in fact, it

makes them look like a pathetic twodge that everyone laughs at behind their backs, and occasionally to their faces.
c.f shreddie **UK (Mid)**

condy boy, adj.

obsolete term for a 'rouseabout' in a brothel. (From the use of Condy's crystal used by prostitutes for cleaning after intercourse.) *Circa* 1940s–50s **AUS**

cooney, n.

the malicious practice of running up behind your victim, and punching him in the testicles whilst screaming 'Cooney!' before running off. *f.* This was a common 80s practise in E. Midlands (UK) following boxer Gerry Cooney's infamous scrotal blow on poor Larry Holmes in 1981/2. **UK (Mid) (Wal)**

cootch, n.

woman's genital area *f.* This word raises all sorts of interesting possibilities since the old Welsh word 'cwtch' (which has a similar pronunciation) is often used to mean a 'place of comfort'. It makes me wonder if the word was carried to the states by Welsh immigrants then mutated and adopted by people who would have no idea of its origins. **USA (S)**

cooties, n.

initially introduced as a bug – probably head lice – cooties are some form of horrid affliction that you can get by coming into contact with anyone of the opposite sex, or sometimes same sex, if they're gross. (i.e. all gross people by definition have cooties.)

So once established as an imaginary infestation on the playground, cooties have become to be associated almost exclusively with girls (possibly because they traditionally have more hair for head lice to infest) although anyone of questionable hygiene is subject to cootie ridicule. Either way, for boys the rule is 'Stay away from girls, because girls have cooties'.

Infestation could be prevented by common measures like crossing your fingers or simply by avoiding contact with infected persons (i.e. running away as fast as you can). Also you could receive a cootie immunization by the well-known incantation and actions:

> 'Circle, Circle, dot, dot, dot
> Now I have my cootie shot'

(whilst drawing 2 circles on your forearm, and then poking it three times in the middle for the dot, dot, dot part), I'm sure there is a lot more cootie lore out there *Circa* 1940s+
USA

cowabunga, n.
(1) It's like... 'Oh, my God!' 'Wow!' 'I'm impressed!' While used in the *Teenage Mutant Ninja Turtles* books/movies/etc., the expression goes back at least to the late 1940s with the *Howdy Doody* television program, where it was used quite often as an expression of surprise.
(2) common use is as a 'shout' made just before a charge... similar to Geronimo! *f.* (currently) the Teenage Mutant Ninja Turtles **USA**

cow juice, n.
milk. Given away free in schools until Mrs Thatcher became Minister of Education. Produced the 'rhyme' 'Maggie Thatcher milk snatcher, Thatcher Snatcher Baby Basher'. 'Thatcher Snatcher' has stayed as one of the venerable Baroness's nicknames ever since. **UK**

crabs, n.
body lice, usually now restricted to describe the variety that specialises in infesting the pubic areas (yes, they DO specialise) *c.f.* Nitty Nora **USA**

crafty butcher, n.
homosexual, so called because he takes meat through the back door.

craft and daft, n.
more commonly known as the technical subject 'craft & design' **UK (Scot)**

craphole commando, n.
commonly used to describe a homosexual. Also known as poof, jobby jabber, uphill gardener, chutney ferret, brown spoon boy, chocolate boat floater, etc *Circa* 2000 **UK**

crater-face, n.
term used to describe someone with really bad acne or similar **UK**

cree, n.
Gives immunity in a game. Crossing fingers and shouting 'cree' made you neutral until the game restarted. Used in Monmouthshire and other places in Wales in the thirties and forties and still in use today *c.f.* barley's, fainites *Circa* 1930s-current **UK (W, Wal)**

cretin, n.
originally a medical term denoting a specific level of mental impairment, this is now used mainly as a derogatory term for a unpleasant or unintelligent person. 'Oi, you cretin'. A really dumb, nasty person is a 'stupid cretin' *Circa* 1960+
UK (Wal)

crezzer, n.
scrubber, tramp, tart. Possible derived from 'Crescent', as in Halton Moor Crescent in Leeds. For some reason, council estates in Leeds have more than their fair share of crescents, which usually aren't even crescent-shaped! **UK (N)**

croggie/croggy/crozzy, n.
giving someone a lift on the back of your bike *c.f.* backy **UK (NE)**

crossie, v.
an often painful way of giving someone a lift on the handlebar of your bike, preventing you from clearly seeing oncoming lamp-posts and foot high curbs *Circa* 1940+ **UK (Scot)**

crotch cutters, n.
short shorts, hot pants *Circa* 2000 **USA**

crumbles/crumblies, n.
dog shit – the kind that goes white when dry and crumbles when you fall on it **UK (Wal)**

crusty, n.
(1) To run up behind someone when they weren't looking and rap them on the top of their head with your knuckles as hard as you could. You would then shout, 'Crusty', and run off
(2) traveller, gypsy, beggar or anyone who looked particularly 'dirty'
Circa 1980s-90s **UK (SW)**

cuffy, adj.
badly dressed. A wearer of outdated style of clothing. To say someone was cuffy was the worst possible thing you could say to them. It meant they had no dress sense – e.g. wore

trousers that had obviously been hand-me-downs from their brother, especially flares. For a brief while, those parka coats with fur round the hood were the ultimate fashion no-no, and wearing one condemned you to face life as a cuffy. In some areas it was also used to indicate a child didn't wash too regularly *Circa* 1984 **UK (Wal)**

curbs, n.
ball game where two people stand on either side of a road, and throw a football across in turn, trying to get the ball to 'bounce' into the opposing curb and therefore ricochet up in the air (or in the best cases, ricochet straight back across the road to the thrower's side, allowing them to get another go) Winner was first to 10 'curbs' **UK (NE)**

'cutting a rusty', ph.
describes the result of a small child making a mess in their nappy (diaper) and smelling up the whole room. Used as 'Dang Lurlene – it stinks in here. That young 'un must have cut a rusty!' Originated 'down South' and used by women and men in trailer parks all over *Circa* 1990s
USA

D

Daaaaave..., n.
used to a friend to indicate they'd done something a bit stupid. Pronounced in slow-mo as if talking to someone a bit thick. Generally it's quite an affectionate term. Apparently Germans use the name 'Jurgen' to identical effect *Circa* 1990s **UK**

daks, n.
underdaks, underpants **AUS**

dags, n.
(1) the small (sometimes large) solid lumps of manure hanging from a sheep's wool around their rear ends where their droppings have fouled it *c.f.* winnets, arsenuts, cleggs, klingons
(2) an excessively annoying or unpleasant person **AUS**

dancing dollies, n.
a typically sadistic playground game in which several targets lined up against a wall whilst others attempted to hit them with spherical projectiles (commonly tennis, golf and footballs, less commonly a cricket ball), creating the appearance of 'dancing', in the targets, when avoiding the missiles. Popular in spring/summer terms at primary schools *Circa* 1980s **UK (NW)**

danger wank, n.

thrill-seeking masturbation, while your mum is walking upstairs to your bedroom after you have called her. The object of the game is to come before she opens the door and catches you *Circa* 2002 **UK (SE)**

dangleberries, n.

the little bits of dried jobbie hanging on to your bumfluff *c.f.* dags, winnets, etc.**UK (Scot)**

deacon, n.

derog. An excessively stupid or unpleasant person. *f.* JOEY DEACON, elderly man suffering from cerebral palsy regularly featured on television 1980-85 *c.f.* joey, spack, spaz

dee-bee, n.

term used where ever a group of lads would congregate and only one had any cigarettes. As soon as this lad lit or 'sparked up' his cigarette, the others would vie for a Dee-Bee meaning 'Decent Butt'. If you were unable to secure Dee Bee, you would then have to appeal for Dee-Dee-Bee and so on.

It was also used to demonstrate your place in the hierarchy; if you ended with the lip-burning soggy last drag, which was more often than not mainly filter, it was a sure sign that you were not the most popular or hardest member of the group *Circa* 1980s **UK (Mid)**

dee-bo, n.

(1) Acknowlegement someone has delivered a telling insult or response. e.g.

Kid 1:	Can have some of that candy?'
Kid 2:	'When pigs fly!'
Bystander:	'DEE-BO'.

(2) sports trash talk: exclamation after stealing the ball, reject-

ing a shot, etc *Circa* Jan 2000 **USA (Seat.)**

deefer, n.
school prefect. Probably mutated rhyming slang *f.* deefer = defect = prefect

defo/double damn defo, adj.
abbr. of definitely. Double damn defo was an extension of defo (definitely) to indicate that it was 'written in stone...' **UK**

derbrain, n.
See durbrain.

derbenny, n.
derbenny is interchangeable with durbrain. It may have something to do with Benny off *Crossroads* being such a twat and thus a good thing to call someone *Circa* 1978-81 **UK (SW)**

dibber-dobber, n.
someone who tells tales on you. The school chant for this sort of person was 'Dibber-dobbers wear nappies' and was considered a strong defence to the threats of the class tattle-tale *Circa* 1980s **AUS**

dibs, n.
shouting this word is laying claim to something; the last cookie, the best seat, the right to go first in a game **USA**

dick, n.
penis *Circa* 1800+ **UK**

dick eye, n.
insult usually said to males by males. Imaginative offensive

put-down using part of male anatomy *Circa* 2001 **UK**

dickhead, n.
a stupid person, or one behaving stupidly

dickup, exc.
a shout: translates into 'Attention, attention; a teacher is approaching. Extinguish your cigarettes immediately.' Usually accompanied by teacher nickname e.g. 'Dickup, Crogger!' **UK (SE)**

dickies, n.
head lice *c.f.* nits, cooties **UK (NE)**

dickie head, n.
child suffering from head lice *c.f.* nitty nora **UK (NE)**

dicksplash, adj.
person of diminished intelligence or capability. e.g. applied to a person who performs an act incorrectly *c.f.* joey, spazmo etc **UK**

dickwad/dickweed, adj.
insult. Similar in use to dickhead *Circa* 1980s **USA**

diesel, adj.
(1) beer
(2) refers to someone 'tough and strong'. 'He's really diesel...!'
AUS, USA (Virg)

dingbat, adj.
fool or idiot. Pos. Australian derivative of ding? *Circa* 1960s+ **AUS**

dingie, v.

to stand someone up or ignore them (pronounced ding-ghee). Used as 'He pure dingied me, by the way ...', or when someone unsuccessfully attempts to pull a member of the opposite sex, their friends would all shout 'dingied!' *c.f.* pie *Circa* 1980s–current **UK (Scot)**

dinky-di, adj.

correct, good, favourable *c.f.* dinkum **AUS**

dinkum, adj.

good, reliable honest. When used with 'fair', it can be a query regarding authenticity e.g. 'Is that fair dinkum?' **AUS**

dinner grannies, n.

fairly obvious name for dinner ladies – school canteen staff who were almost always of a certain age. They were almost always evil too, and despised children. Main role was to be tyrannical at dinner times when they had the job of maintaining order throughout the school. This was generally achieved by stealing the tennis balls that people were playing football with (casey's being banned on the tarmac). It was the duty of a dinner granny to confiscate any ball or playground equipment (conkers etc) that may come their way. Such confiscation was nearly always permanent *c.f.* casey, *Circa* 1980s-90s **UK (NE)**

dipping, v.

selection process determining who was/wasn't 'it', prior to a game of tug/tag/whatever. The participants would put their feet in a circle and someone would point in turn whilst reciting a short rhyme, moving round the circle with each word, or syllable, depending on the rhyme or, often, the dipper's fancy e.g.

'Ip-dip, cow shit
hanging on the line
wind blew, shit flew
out pops...you.'

In this case, the owner of the 14th foot pointed to would be removed from the circle and the process repeated until only one was left and they were 'it' (nb. 'on the' counted or only one move, for some reason) An alternative ending was:

'...out pops
Y.O.U.
are
it!'

UK (NE)

dipstick, n.
daft person *c.f.* divvy **UK (NW)**

dirk/derk/durk, n.
dirk was used in exactly the same way as knob is this these days, i.e. 'You stupid dirk!' Used when you didn't have time or energy to pronounce all the syllables in longer more insulting words (which were probably a bit gay and not at all insulting really – well, for 5–8-year-olds, that is) you would call them a dirk. **UK (Wal)**

dirty sanchez, n.
the act of giving your 'intercourse partner' a moustache made of their own faeces *Circa* 2000
USA

div/divvy/divot, n.
derog. An excessively stupid or unpleasant person. *f.* clod or

73

divot of turf or earth

dob, dob in, v.
to 'tell tales', report misdemeanours to teachers, parents or police **AUS**

dobber, n.
(1) a glass marble of around 25mm in diameter, and so around twice the size of the more usual sized variety.
(2) a condom (term popularly used in Leicester and Surrounds.
3) In the Derby area of the UK during the 50s and 60s this was the popular name for a catapult – does this suggest that the folks in Leicester were hard put to find elastic for their weapons? *c.f.* blob *Circa* mid 1980s **UK**

dockers, v.
to claim rights to consumption of 'left-over' food or drink when the original owner has had sufficient. Used as 'dockers on your bifta?', 'dockers on your fag?', 'dockers on your ale', etc. Should be used in question form but the first few words, i.e. 'Can I have … ', is usually left off. The claim is usually finished with the word laird (which means lad). Hence user shouting 'No dockers, no nothing, no greedy scavs' just before opening a packet of crisps, or whatever, to prevent people stealing them *c.f.* scavs *Circa* 1980s – onwards **UK (NW)**

dog, v.
to 'dog it' was to abscond from school for the day – or however long took your fancy. A day would often begin with friends asking each other if they were 'dogging' it today. Sometimes people larger than you forced you to dog it with them (just in case anyone thought they were unpopular...) Whilst doing so, you were often chased by a man from the

local council education dept. (the 'dogger man') who happened to have some advantage over you as you were on foot, and he was in his 'dogger van'. Used in West of Scotland – Lanarkshire. **UK (Scot)**

dog pile, n.

yelled out joyfully, this term causes any child, especially boys, to look about, see who's down, and pile on top of them. Frequently occurred in casual football games, but happened any time a person went to the ground *c.f.* pile on
UK

d'oh, n.

expression of displeasure after an unfortunate event. Popularised by Homer from *The Simpsons Circa* 1990s
UK, USA, AUS

'doing a loony', ph.

person taunted so much they retaliate violently. Also described as chucking a mental, copping the strop, or spitting the dummy.

doley, adj.

someone whose only means of subsistence is the money paid to them by the state to avoid hardship because they are unable or unwilling to work. The obvious trappings of poverty such as 'clothes by Tesco' were a constant source of amusement to those children who were lucky enough to have slightly more affluent parents *Circa* 1970–90 **UK**

done, v.

to get 'done' means to be told off or chastised for some wrong-doing e.g. 'I got done for pulling her hair!' *Circa* 1980s
UK (NE)

donkey, n.
an excessively stupid or unpleasant person.

donald duck, rh.

> Donald Duck did some muck
> On the kitchen floor.
> Daisy Duck licked it up
> And Donald did some more.

Circa 1980s **UK (Mid)**

donk, n.
idiot, usually large in size and very clumsy. The funniness incurred stems from the onomatopoeic quality of the word donk and relation to the word donkey. Can be said repeatedly in a low voice for extra funniness 'DONK DONK DONK DONK'
(Ed: which is actually funnier in practice than in print)
Circa 1990s **UK**

dookie, n.
excrement, poo, faeces, i.e. shit **USA**

doofus, n.
an exceptionally thick person or used as an insult for someone who has just done something particularly silly. **USA**

dope hoe, n.
describes a prostitute paid for sex with drugs (usu. marijuana or cocaine). Children use it as an insult to someone, 'Shut up Darcy, you're such a dope hoe'. Similar to crack whore
Circa 1990s **USA**

dopper, n.
person of diminished intelligence, i.e. div, cretin
Circa 1982 – 87 **UK (SE)**

dork, n.
(1) penis
(2) an excessively stupid or irritating person (often to be found wearing an anorak at the end of platforms noting down the serial numbers of trains)

doss bag, n.
an exceptionally lazy person

douche bag, n.
an unattractive or offensive person, often old. *f.* named after the device females use to clean their vaginas after sexual intercourse

double bass, adj.
A sexual position in which the man enters the woman from behind, and then fiddles with the woman's nipples with one hand and her budgie's tongue with the other. The position is similar to that used when playing a double bass instrument, but the sound produced is slightly different *c.f.* budgie's tongue **AUS**

double click (... your mouse), n.
techno-influenced word for female masturbation **AUS**

doug, n.
Alone. Generated from a kid whose nickname was Doug – and had no friends. He was so notorious that it soon passed into common usage, as in 'He's on his doug', 'Don't go on your doug, wait for me' and 'He's been douged'. Has also come to mean someone is scruffily dressed and acts like a

general tramp *Circa* 1994 onwards **UK (Wal)**

dougie/duggie, adj.
Exceptionally thick person. Interchangeable with spacker/spanner, but perhaps slightly less offensive *Circa* 1980s **UK (NE)**

drive, n.
generic title for anyone who drives for a living, (i.e taxi, bus driver etc) e.g. 'Cheers drive' when disembarking **UK (Wal)**

'drain the main vein', ph.
to urinate in a particularly speedy manner (probably to avoid being caught doing it in a public place) e.g. in a shop doorway or telephone box on the way home from the pub *Circa* 1940s to date **AUS**

dresser, n.
supposedly a football hooligan gang in mid 80s Newcastle that many pupils aspired to belong to. Similar to the 'Casuals' of Edinburgh, although there is no direct evidence that they ever actually existed and therefore may have been purely imaginary. However, being described as a 'dresser' was one of the highest accolades a playground thug could achieve.

The attire of an aspirant dresser consisted of: Farrah 'dress pants', black flecked with red and yellow; pastel shaded Lacoste polo shirt; coloured 'sea-sider' deck shoes; and Barber waxed jacket. On school days the Lacoste would have to be substituted for a white nylon job with the tie done up in as big a knot as possible, rather like some plebeian cravat. The look is best described as a proto-Alan Partridge effect *Circa* 1980s **UK (Scot)**

drongo, n.

fool, simpleton, slow learner, 'hopeless case'. *Circa* 1940s to date **AUS**

'drop the kids off', ph.

to produce faeces. Used as in 'I'm just popping to the bathroom... gotta drop the kids off, if y'know what I mean.' *c.f.* release the hounds, clip a steamer

'dropping bottom', ph.

driving around with the bass on the audio system set at a vibration level liable to cause permanent damage to hearing and possibly other internal organs. Or to put it another way, 'Yo dude just chillin' round town dropping bottom.'

To elucidate, dropping bottom is dumping extreme amounts of low frequencies into the stratosphere. i.e. big subwoofers in a automobile *Circa* 1990s **USA**

duck's disease, n.

to have short legs, i.e. having one's bum too close the floor

dude, n.

(1) general term for almost any person

(2) used as 'skill' with similar response that the person who had said 'dude' is promptly to be told that a 'dude' was actually the arse hair of a camel *c.f.* skill **UK**

duff over/duff up, v.

to strike, hit or 'beat up'. e.g. 'let's duff him over' **UK**

dur-brain, n.

'excessively stupid person'. Insult usually combined with pushing your tongue between your lower lip and teeth (as with 'spazmo' etc) and making an 'eeerrrrrr' sound (easier to do than describe). Can be shortened to simply 'dur' *c.f.* minda *Circa* 1970-80 **UK (SW)**

dullion/dul-yon, n.

used as an exclamation upon executing a particularly violent and/or effective and/or demonstrative act on another, mostly unsuspecting person or upon seeing such an act perpetrated on a third party.

For example; third year dinner hall, St. Ninians' High School Giffnock. Stephen Brown (or 'Broono') scones Kenneth Baird (or 'Buffer') with a lunch tray full square on the back producing a dull sound usually associated with slapping the side of an empty oil drum. As Buffer collapsed into a heap amongst the slops Broono roared, 'That was a fuckin' dullion!' and was answered with cries from the attendant muckers of 'Fuckin' dullion man!'

dumps, n.

Glaswegian version of the bumps (birthday celebration) involving back-punching and bum-kneeing *c.f.* bumps
UK (Scot)

dung trumpet, n.

anus, or bum-hole. Used for example as 'Right up the dung trumpet' (with heavy emphasis on the word 'right') *Circa* 1990s **UK**

dunny, n.

toilet (originally outside but now any): e.g. the classic 'Aussie curse': i.e. 'may your chooks turn into emus and kick your dunny down!'

There is an ongoing theme in Australian urban mythology about the redback spider that hides under the toilet seat and leaps out to bite yer bum (or worse) when you go to satisfy nature's urges. Tales abound of men leaping from the seat clutching their nadgers and begging someone to suck the poison out – though many think this is merely a thinly-veiled request for oral sex.

In fact this is based on reality as in 'the old days', few homes had indoor plumbing and most used outdoor dunnys (*a la Shrek*) which was basically a hole in the ground with an improvised seat over it. Redback spiders like dark moist conditions which the dunny provided, and the crap attracted flies which of course was an ideal food supply. Therefore the old style dunny was an ideal place for these things to live. You won't find too many of them indoors, though, so using the loo in Australia isn't a dangerous experience – often **AUS**

dustbin kid, n.
derog. a handicapped person, flid *f.* rhyming slang Dustbin Lid *c.f.* flid **UK (SE)**

dutch oven, n.
to fart in bed and then quickly pull the covers over your partner's head. *Circa* 1990s **USA**

dylan, n.
a dozy cunt. From the so named hippy rabbit in the *Magic Roundabout*, who was usually asleep. Used as 'Wake up you fucking Dylan, we're going scrumping' *Circa* 1970s **UK**

E

eeearrr, exc.
squealing exclamation uttered when someone unwittingly makes a comment which could be interpreted as being homosexual in nature, or if a pupil (or teacher) of questionable sexuality walked into the room *c.f.* naaarse **UK (SE)**

'edge-of-the-bed-virgin', ph.
teenage girls who regularly entice boys into sexual situations then back out at the last possible moment *c.f.* prickteaser *Circa* 1990s **UK (N)**

edgie/ejji, n.
derogatory term for a poor and unkempt person. Suggests the person receives education benefits. Pertains particularly to cheap school uniforms dished out to kids whose parents couldn't afford decent ones. Consequently it was vitally important to buy blazers etc. which were sufficiently different to 'Edgie' uniforms *Circa* 1990s **UK (Mid)**

edgy (to keep...), v.
call made by the 'lookout person' when others were up to no good. For example, if you're breaking into a house, and a car pulls in the driveway, the lookout person (who would be keeping edgy) shouts, 'Edgy' and everyone would know to run. To keep 'Edgy' you are the lookout person, you will

warn anyone else you are with *Circa* 1990s **UK (Scot)**

edna!, n.
unbelievable. usu. used as an insult and combined with fero-
cious rubbing of the chin (a la Jimmy Hill), usually administered to some kid who says his dad plays for Liverpool.
c.f. chinny reck-on, moose *Circa* 1980–84 **UK (NW)**

eejit, n.
idiot. Term popularised in the UK by the annoying Irish
expatriot television and radio 'personality' Terry Wogan
Circa 1990s **UK**

egg-bound, adj.
to be constipated due to eating too many eggs.
*(Ed:Included, because it's such a nice word – regardless of
whether eggs DO cause constipation or not)* *Circa* 1800s+ **UK**

e.l.f., ph.
'eighties live forever'. Used to describe someone who has not
yet moved on from plaid and other fashion don'ts. 'That guy
is such an ELF!' *Circa* 1990s **UK**

elm, n.
stupid, lame, crap person. Used as 'You elm'. This may have
been specific to the contributor's school as it started the summer they cut down all the Elm trees thanks to Dutch Elm
Disease, and their field was left with stumps of rotting trees...
an obvious name for someone useless, then *Circa* 1977 **UK
(Mid)**

elton, n.
toilet. Play on words Elton 'John' *Circa* 1980s **UK**

empty, adj.

when someone free of any markers during a game of play-ground football. For example, a call of 'I'm empty' would suggest that that person is unmarked and in a good position to shoot *Circa* 1990s **UK**

endo, n.

BMX stunt involving applying brakes hard to the front wheel causing the rear to lift as high as possible in the air. Ideally performed inches in front of least hard of available mates *c.f.* BMX, mongoose, the ramp.

ennit/innit, n.

version of yes or yeah. Commonly used amongst and prima-rily by Native American Individuals who do possess a large vocabulary of various dialects of Native American languages but choose to simplify languages so that the average person can comprehend them. This word is currently used on and around Federally-recognized reservations in the Midwest now. It has been used for years and has no definite origins that are commonly known.

Word also used in UK (esp. South) by males/females in Kappa tracksuits with mobile phones, and is said after every sentence. Used by those with a small vocabulary *f.* is it not?, isn't it? **USA, UK**

en-og, n.

term for alleyway (entry) between houses. Often really scum-my nasty place full of dog crap – it was a bit of an initiation to pee in a new en-og.**UK (NW)**

eppy, n.

(1) a person (usu. child) suffering from epilepsy
(2) an epileptic fit
(3) a fit of temper

(4) an excessively stupid or unpleasant person *c.f.* spack, flid, joey

ernskernabernaferna, n.
A word to use when a teacher looks at you and says your name. You can look at him or her like you don't know what's going on and say 'ernskernabernaferna' and look stupid; this word is just basically saying 'What?' but in a funny way which annoys the teacher. Pronunciation 'Ern-is-ker-na-burn-na-fur-na' *Circa* 1990s **UK**

etch-a-sketch, n./v.
(1) children's toy on which kids draw erasable pictures
(2) the act of trying to draw a smile on a woman's face by twiddling both of her nipples simultaneously

evil, n.
a 'extreme' frown. A dirty look e.g. 'He was giving me evils' *Circa* 1990s **UK (SE)**

exypesh, adj.
extremely good or favourable. Extra special e.g. 'That game is exypesh like.' *Circa* 1990s

F

'face like a bag of arses', ph.
ugly *Circa* 1990s **EIRE**

'face like a leper licking piss off a thistle', ph.
usually used to describe an ugly girl. Similar to saying someone 'has a face like a bulldog chewing a wasp' **UK (E, Mid)**

fag tag, n.
seemingly pointless 'loop' on the back of a boy's/man's 'Oxford' type shirt. Many kids were caught pulling loops off victims *Circa* 1970s **UK (SE)**

fainites barley, ph.
expression which, when shouted, gives you protection and prevents attack during games of touch such as British Bulldog etc *c.f.* fleas-inject, faynights, skinchies **UK**

family jewels, n.
male genitalia *c.f.* wedding tackle, meat and two veg **UK**

fanny batter, n.
term for general lubrication provided by a woman's genitalia (fanny). If you had managed to get 'fingers' off a girl you'd often waggle them under the noses of your mates, ask what they could smell and they'd shout 'eeurgh, fanny batter'

Circa 1970s **UK (S. Wal.)**

fanny-fart, n.
noise caused by escape of trapped air from vagina during or after coitus *Circa* 1980s **UK (SE)**

fanny flaps, n.
labia *c.f.* piss flaps

fark, exc.
variation on pronunciation of 'fuck' usually used as an expression of disbelief or objection. 'Oh faaarrrk ... my pen's broke!' *Circa* 1970s **UK**

'farmers in the meadow...', poem
Similar to the others of this genre – and sharing some of the words:

> Farmer's in the meadow, mowing all his grass,
> Along came a bee and stung him on the
> Ask no questions, tell no lies,
> I saw a doctor doing up his
> Flies are a nuisance, bees are worse,
> I saw a doctor chatting up a
> Nurse your children good and well,
> And that is the end of my silly little tale

c.f. Arsehole song (and others) *Circa* 1980s **UK**

fart, v.
to break wind *c.f.* guff

fart-arse, v.
when somebody fart-arses around they waste time, or only put in half the effort. For example, 'He did a fart-arsed job

and I had to do it again after he finished!', or 'Will you stop fart-arsing and come here?' **AUS**

fart knocker, n.

stupid person, jerk. Reported to us as one of Beavis and Butthead's many wonderful insults but now claimed to be in use as early as 1974 when contributor was in kindergarten. He still uses it as a nostalgic reference to someone who was a complete moron *Circa* 1990s **USA**

fat pastie, v.

used as substitute for fat bastard. Can be said it front of teachers and it almost gets you into trouble until they realise what you said *Circa* 1990s **UK**

Fatty and Skinny, rh.

Fatty and Skinny went to the Zoo
Fatty got lost in the elephants' poo
Skinny went home to tell his mum
But all he got was a smack on the bum,

Also this from contributor who says the rhyme was in use before the 1970s:

Fatty and Skinny sleeping in the bed.
Fatty rolled over, now Skinny's dead.

Circa 1960s–80s **UK**

faynights/fainites, exc.

a 'shout' (often accompanied by crossed fingers) created temporary immunity from being made 'it' when playing sticky toffee, stuck in the mud, tag, etc *c.f.* skinchies **UK (NE)**

felch/felching, v.

impossible to describe tactfully. Felching is the incredibly grotesque act of orally extracting semen from someone's anus after anal intercourse without a condom. Generally used as a derogatory statement about homosexuals e.g. 'that guy is a real root smoocher, I bet he felches, too' *Circa* 1980s **USA (W)**

fencing, v.

describes a vicious and nasty punishment for 'first year' boys where they were lifted by all four limbs and repeatedly slammed into the end of a fence in the school playground so that the fence hit them between the legs *Circa* 1985 **UK (SE)**

ferret face, n.

insult aimed at someone with 'precious' beard and/or moustache growth **UK (NE)**

felt, adj

term of abuse to describe a person from a poor family: you know, Tesco trainers, Oxfam clothes, smelt bad and always, always seemed to eat egg sandwiches which added to the general bad aroma! *c.f.* pikey **UK (SW)**

fezzer, n.

a fezzer is a Ford Fiesta car. All Ford Fiester's are called Fezzers in Essex, UK. Especially by Gary-boys and Kev's *Circa* 1990s **UK (SE)**

f.h.b., n.

term used in Sandbach School, Cheshire, UK for 'future head boy' – a real swotty sucker destined to be headmaster's favourite chum boy **UK (SE)**

fighty time, n.

cautionary announcement that mass wrestling is to commence at break-time. **UK (SE)**

finger, v.

a post-pubescent (usu.) behind the bike sheds favourite pastime. Involves inserting your finger(s) into the genitalia of
female (if willing). Act often followed by the 'fingerer' running over to his mates and inviting them to 'Smell my fingers
!' as proof of having done the dirty deed *c.f.* fish fingers
UK

finger puppet audition, v.

masturbation **UK**

fink, n./v.

someone who rats on a friend or another child by passing
information relating to a misdemeanour of some sort to an
adult e.g. 'You rat-fink!' (a supposedly more mature term).
As verb e.g. 'You finked on me!' *c.f.* tattle-tale **USA**

fireball, n.

a brand of gob-stopper (sweet). A largish gob-stopper laced
with cayenne that became quite hot after a while. **UK**

fire pie, n.

referring to ginger, or red-head's pubic hair, mostly in the
cases of females *Circa* 1990s **USA**

fish, n.

derog. a surrealist insulting name for an excessively stupid or
unpleasant person **UK (SE)**

fish bits, n.

the long bits of hair at the back of a mullet hairstyle *c.f.* mullet **UK (SE)**

fish fingers, adj.

name given to person who 'fingers' girls but neglects to wash that 'boiled anchovy' smell off his hands afterwards. **UK**

five-finger-discount, n.

stealing, usu. shoplifting **AUS**

five-finger-spread, n.

highly counter-productive attempt to suppress vomit with the hand. Introduced unceremoniously to the English language by ex-pat Aussie, Barry McKenzie, in his infamous but brilliantly funny comic strip published in *Private Eye* *c.f.* hughie *Circa* 1960s **AUS, UK**

five-oh, n.

police: five-oh means 50, used as the TV show *Hawaii 50*. It means cops, police, law enforcement. Ghetto slang for the police. 'I hope the five-oh doesn't read this' **USA**

flabby labby, n.

exceptionally large and 'floppy' vaginal entrance *Circa* 1980s **UK (Mid)**

flasher, n.

person (usu. male) who wears a long mac which he whips open to expose his genitals to women and young children – esp. girls **UK (W)**

'flat out like a lizard drinking', ph.

extremely lazy. Note: Lizards aren't known for their high levels of water consumption *Circa* Current **AUS**

fleabag n.

derog. smelly person dressed in Oxfam style dress, possibly

wearing Tesco trainers, possibly having fleas too *c.f.* stig
UK (SE)

flea dart, n.
wild grass found on school playing fields, usually with fleas
resident. Plucked and thrown at poor children to emphasise
their lack of worth *Circa* 1970s **UK**

fleckie, n.
a fleckie was a nasty description of a working class hooligans
with a fondness for shiny tracksuits. Used as 'that bloke's a
fleckie'. A school bus to a bad school could be termed 'fleck
express' *Circa* 1980s–90s **EIRE**

fleggy/fleg, n.
spit which includes mucus e.g. a 'greeny' e.g. 'I just flegged
in that'; 'You've got a fleggy on the back of your coat' *Circa*
1970s **UK (N)**

fleas-inject, game.
variation of 'It', where you were given the fleas and had to
catch up with someone else and touch them to pass them on.
When you touched them you shouted 'fleas', and then immediately slapped your hand to your opposite upper arm and
shouted 'inject' so that they couldn't get you back.

flid, n.
derog.
1) a person (usu. a child) suffering from birth defects due to
the drug Thalidomide *f.* THALID-omide
2) an excessively stupid or unpleasant person *c.f.* spack,
eppy, joey **UK**

flob, n./v.
1) saliva

92

2) to spit *c.f.* gob, snot, meaty, yocker, semi-phlegmy **UK**

flob race, n.
popular pastime where masses of Fruit Pastilles are consumed to generate a long trail of saliva, which has to reach as close as possible to the ground and then be sucked back up into the mouth. **UK (SE)**

flop one, v.
to masturbate (males) e.g. 'She'd really turned him on so he had to flop one out before he could drop off to sleep.' **USA**

flotch, n.
term used to describe the faecal deposits residing in one's underpants *c.f.* skidmark *Circa* 1970s+ **UK (Mid)**

flube tube, n.
'Flube Tube' used to cover the distinctive aroma of marijuana smoke by blowing into a cardboard tube stuffed with tissue paper *c.f.* spoof tube **USA**

'flying low', ph.
make someone aware that their trouser zip was undone. Used to help resolve a regular schoolboy's accidental occurrence *Circa* 1970s **UK**

fly goalie, n.
situation where anyone in a football team can be a goalkeeper *c.f.* skeleton goalie, *Circa* 1970s–80s
UK (SE)

fother mucker, n.
a marginally less offensive of saying mother-fucker. Whether using it instead of the original will save your teeth is another question *Circa* current **USA (NY)**

four-eyes/double-glazing, n.
tart rejoinder to those with specs

freckle, n.
anus (descriptive) **AUS**

freestand, n.
BMX stunt. Involves standing on the bike frame whilst the bike is in motion. For ultimate cool the rider would stand in crucifix position.

'free the tadpoles', ph.
masturbate, 'liberate' the residents of wank tanks **UK**

frig, v.
though still considered a 'vulgar' word denoting the sexual act, it is nonetheless a slightly more polite way of saying 'fuck'; e.g. 'Go frig yourself!'. Often used by 'ladies' to show how genteel they are! Can also mean 'to finger' *Circa* current **UK**

frigmarole, n.
unnecessarily time-consuming foreplay **UK**

front bottom, n.
female genital area including vagina. Felt to be a less offensive mode of reference than, for example, 'cunt' *c.f.* twat, muff, quim etc.

frosty, n.
to 'give someone a frosty' meant to run up behind them on the school field (after some heavy snow) and pile as much snow and ice right down their back as you could manage. Used as 'I'm going to give him a frosty at lunchtime'. More vicious frosties involved just pushing the person over into

the snow and jumping up and down on them until they suf-
focated or lost consciousness *Circa* 1980s **UK**

fruit-cup, v.
oral sex on male where woman stimulates the scrotum and
testicles *Circa* 1990s **USA**

fubar, ac.
acronym for 'Fucked Up Beyond All Recognition'. Used in
WW2 to describe a desperate situation. Now used in almost
any situation generally towards a person that one dislikes, or,
just like in the past, towards/about a really shitty situation
Circa 1940s+ **USA, UK**

'fucking-A', ph.
objection. When one is really fed up with something they
sometimes proclaim, 'Fucking-A man!' or somewhere along
those lines *Circa* 2000 **USA**

'fucked to a fair-thee-well', ph.
screwed up beyond recognition *Circa* 1980s–90s **USA**

fucknut, n.
An excessively stupid or unpleasant person **NZ**

fucknuckle, n.
A stupid clumsy or unpleasant person **AUS**

fuck the dog/dog-fucker, v./n.
to waste time, to avoid work. A dog-fucker is someone who
'fucks the dog'. i.e. avoids work, labour *Circa* 1990 **CAN**

fudge-nudger, n.
male homosexual *Circa* 2001+ **UK**

'fuggedaboudit', ph.

contraction of 'Forget About It', as in 'Should I worry about that?', 'Nah, fuggedaboudit' *Circa* 1980+ **USA**

fugly, n.

an unattractive person. Contraction of 'Fucking ugly!' **UK**

fun bags, n.

female breasts *Circa* 1980s **USA (S)**

fur burger, n.

the female genitalia

fweep, v.

to fweep someone is to smack their dangly bits. Almost exclusively used for guys, because girls don't have anything to fweep. Generally the fweeper will be standing next to his victim and suddenly backhand the poor guy **USA (MW)**

G

gank, v.
to steal. Used as 'He ganked their stereo', 'I'm gonna gank that CD – keep tabs for me?' *Circa* 2000 **USA**

gantin, v.
'She was fair gantin for a shag but I wisnae gonnae knob that mingin hoor. Literally 'gaping' (or possibly 'gasping') now used in the same sense as 'gagging'. Origin: Old Scots *Circa* 1900+ **UK (Scot)**

gardener, n.
person of low intellect. This was used at the contributor's school due to the fact that the thickest kids (in stream five) did a subject termed 'Rural Studies' instead of the usual curriculum; this was basically gardening. Gardeners did enjoy some perks such as their own shed in which they smoked and kept extensive porno mag collections *Circa* 1980s **UK**

gary boy, n.
boy racer. Someone who spends lots of money on making their car look good. Has tinted windows and a very loud sound system and drives round and round the town centre day and night. Lots of these 'Gary boys' can be found in Essex. Gary boys are similar to kevs *Circa* 1995 **UK (SE)**

gas bomb, n.

used to describe the act of sitting on a hard surface (often a garden wall or playground floor) to delay the imminent force of the need for a 'number 2'. 'I'm going to do a gas bomb'.

Gas bombs usually lasted from 1 to 5 minutes, until the offending sensation had subsided. This would often give you about 20 minutes more play before the need for the toilet or another (often increasingly harder to contain) gas bomb. A successful gas bomb would normally be met with the expression 'I've caved it', implying the offending number 2 had been forced into hibernation for a while.

An unsuccessful gas bomb does not warrant description *c.f.* turtle's head *Circa* 1980s **UK**

gash, n.

female genitalia, as in 'That girl's trash – she'll flash her gash for cash!' *Circa* 1990s **UK**

gas pedal, v.

when two people are fighting (usually girls) and one is down on the ground on their back, and the other person pulls their legs up in the air and kicks them in between the legs. **UK**

gay, n./adj.

(1) homosexual *Circa* 1970s onwards
(2) nothing to do with homosexuality, but anything that doesn't work right, especially to do with computer games or general entertainment. Also when people cheat online or a game 'lags up' (suffers from internet delays) e.g. 'that was gay'. Also anything inconvenient, unfashionable or disappointing. Used in place of 'this/that sucks' or is 'this/that is uncool' and is used mostly by Middle School and High School students e.g. 'We have to write a five page essay!' 'That is so gay!' *Circa* 1970s+ **UK, USA**

Gaylord, n.
derog. Lord of homosexuals **UK (SE)**

geddit, n.
a request for feedback (not compulsory) in an informal way.
UK

geen, v.
to 'hoik' or 'flob' mucus. Used as 'Some cunt's geened on the
back of my jacket!' Contraction of 'green one' *Circa* 1990s
UK (Scot)

gender bender, n.
transvestite (pos.) homosexual. *f.* popularised by Boy George
and his band Culture Club during the 1980s. **UK (SE)**

genie song, rh.

> I'm a big fat genie
> With a ten foot weenie
> I showed it to the girl next door.
> She thought it was a snake
> So she hit it with a rake
> And now it's only five foot four

USA

genk, n.
Insult denoting excessive book smarts coupled with general
goofy appearance. e.g. 'Stop putting your hand up, you speccy genk'. Nearly always accompanied by the word speccy
(wearing glasses) *Circa* 1980s **UK (NE)**

geoff, n.
someone not quite clever enough to do A-levels. GEF

(General Education Foundation) courses were general, slightly-more-advanced than O-level courses which provided you with a good grounding in flipping burgers or booking holidays. GEF became Geoff as in 'Is he doing A-levels? No he's a Geoff.' **UK (SE)**

george, n.
word used to mean a menstrual period. At Ackworth School, Yorkshire, UK (a Quaker boarding school) the dates of the girls' periods had to be recorded in the 'George Book' *Circa* 1960-70s **UK (NE)**

ghosties, n./exc.
(1) a booger (dried up snot) floating in mid-nostril suspended by nose hair. Most commonly occurring when looking up at a teacher.
(2) in the game of playground handball, when people who were excluded from the game could run about the squares yelling GHOSTIES! and generally disrupt the game. (They were considered invisible because they were ghosts so anyone who hit the ghosties with the ball were out of the game.) *Circa* 1990s **AUS**

giblets, n.
female genitalia *Circa* 2000 **UK**

ging, v.
to cry, weep *Circa* 1900+ **UK (NE)**

ginge/r minger, n.
self-explanatory and was used to refer to people presumed to have ginger coloured pubic hair. The person responsible for this 'crime' was thus referred to as a 'GINGER MINGER'. More interestingly, the phrase survived the trip from Primary

to Secondary education, although with a few notable changes. The pronunciation altered so that the phrase was pronounced with French vowels: 'gonge monge'.

Furthermore at Bishop Vesey's Grammar School, the contributor can remember that the phrase was also used to refer to a particular sort of ginger cake available at school dinners. They had a red-haired hard of hearing dinner lady in charge of cakes, and so much pleasure was derived by asking for this cake by its nickname. Asking the woman: 'Can I have a slice of ginge minge please?' was a phrase so loaded with meaning that at the time it seemed the schoolboy equivalent of Shakespeare *c.f.* fire pie *Circa* 1980-1990s **UK (Mid)**

ginger, n.
male homosexual. From rhyming slang, ginger beer=queer *Circa* 1930s+ **UK**

ginny woman, n.
(pronounced 'jinny') A non-homosexual male who seems to display personality characteristics normally associated with a female. For example he acts 'womanly' or 'wimpy' and/or whines/complains a lot *Circa* 2001 **CAN**

gippo, n.
1) a gypsy
2) Poorly dressed, trashy kid. (also making reference to someone who smells.)

git, n.
(1) an excessively stupid or unpleasant person
(2) term of abuse misinterpreted at West Lodge Middle School, Pinner, Middlesex in late-70s, where rumour circulated that it was the proper scientific term for 'a pregnant camel'. Hence common playground dialogue: 'You git!'. 'Fuck off, I am not a pregnant camel' **UK**

'gladly my cross-eyed bear', ph.

corrupted line from the hymn 'Gladly my cross I'd bear' – which caused much hilarity amongst schoolkids whenever it was announced in Assembly *Circa* 1950-60s **UK**

glaikit, v.

glazed or vacant expression, having the appearance of stupidity. Widely used around Scotland *Circa* 1950s+ **UK (Scot)**

glebe, n.

'Special Needs' kid, a spacker. (orig. local 'special' school in Wallsend, called The Glebe) **UK (NE)**

gnarly, adj.

surfie word with several meanings including: dangerous, rough, out of control, huge, good, bad or ugly *Circa* Current **AUS**

goal-hanging, n.

a primitive form of offside in football. If the other team think you've scored too many goals they have a go at you for goal-hanging and make you go and be goalie (or something equally horrible) **UK**

'goat's in the garden (...eating the grass)', ph.

description of a girl whose pants were so tight that you could supposedly see the fanny flaps through said pants. One would alert others by saying 'Goat's in the garden, eating the grass.' This eventually became shortened to 'Goat's in the garden.' *c.f.* camel toe *Circa* 1985–2000 **USA (SE)**

gob, n./v.

mouth. Also to forcefully expel a mixture of saliva and mucus derived from nasal passages or bronchea, to spit *c.f.* semi-phlegmy, meaty, snot

goffers, n.
name for sweets/toffees. Used (usu.) as 'I'm off to the goffer shop', 'to scam some goffers.' **UK**

gofer, n.
oily unpopular kid who crawled to the 'big kids' by doing whatever they were asked. e.g. 'Go fer this... go fer that...' and the name stuck. **UK (Wal)**

gogona (take a...), n.
evacuate the bowel, crap. Pronounced 'go-go-nuh' *f.* contracted form of 'got to go now' *Circa* 2001 **CAN**

gold label, n.
12% proof beer, which is topped up to a pint with lemonade and consumed by fifteen-year-olds in the backroom of the local 'safe pub' *c.f.* safe pub **UK**

gollop, v.
to eat too fast or hurriedly, hardly tasting the food. Usually used when kids are eating their tea too fast in order to go out and play e.g. your mother shouts 'Don't gollop yer food or I'll mash yer!' **UK (Mid)**

gommo, n.
a popular Midlands variation of spaz, spakker etc – usually performed with the same mock voice with the tongue forced down behind the bottom lip. 'I'm not working with him, he's a fuckin gommo!' Contributor says he thought it seemed at the time to be less derogatory to the disabled than spaz. Only problem was it was always said with the mad voice and the smacking of the back of the hand – so probably just as bad. Possibly Black Country in origin but very, very popular – more so than spakker and joey *c.f.* spaz, spackker, joey, mong *Circa* mid-1980s **UK (Mid)**

gonk, n.

idiotic person, or a person of low intelligence. Used mostly by children. Imagine the hilarities which ensued when a child recently called out 'YOU'RE MEANT TO BE OVER THERE, YOU STUPID FUCKING TWAT-HEAD GONK!' during a game of 'Friendly Football'. *f.* little hairy toys called Gonks **UK (NE)**

googiana, n.

pussy/sex **UK**

gooleys/goolies/goozies, n.

testes *c.f.* tecks, balls, bollocks (etc.)

goozer, n.

person who would try to muscle in on anything anyone else was doing that looked more interesting than what they were doing. Generally, a less popular kid trying to get in with popular kids. *f.* contr. mutation of 'gooseberry' **UK (W)**

goss/gozz, v.

to spit *c.f.* flob **UK (Mid)**

'got your tatties in?', ph.

the phrase means 'have you got any dried bits of poo on your bum?' ('Tatties' pronounced 'tay-tees') Though the contributor has no idea why the phrase was used! *Circa* 1980s
UK (SE)

grammar poof, n.

ubiquitous insult used by kids from various secondary modern schools against Grammar School kids if you were spotted in your uniform. The reply was usually 'Thicko!' if you were in a gang or feeling brave/suicidal/a good runner *Circa* 1980s **UK (NE)**

grannies/grandpas, n.

the bit of fizzy-drink left in the lip of a soft drink can after drinking. Especially referred to when sharing drinks, where the second person to drink would ask the first person to 'take their grannies with them'. The first would then suck up the remainder around the rim.

Seems they're called grannies or grandpas because they're hard to get rid of and hang around like old people. Sometimes also called stragglers *Circa* 1990s **AUS**

gravy strokes, n.

the final part of sexual intercourse where the male ejaculates *c.f.* vinegar strokes **NZ**

greaser, n.

virtually synonymous with 'rocker', this was anyone who preferred to ride the more functional motorbike instead of the less roadworthy but cleaner scooter (Lambretta or Vespa). Riding these machines was supposed to result in the user becoming 'greasy' because of the open engine design, and thereby needing to wear leathers. The 'mods' on the other hand could wear stylish clothes because the engine of the scooter was fully enclosed *c.f.* slider *Circa* 1960s–70s **UK**

'greasing the weasel', ph.

sexual intercourse. If someone is 'greasing the weasel', it means that they are having sex. For example, 'He said he's not coming out coz him and his missus are greasing the weasel.' Dick equals weasel, greasing through sex *Circa* 1990s **USA**

greb/grebo/greebo, n.

dirty, greasy-haired, pos. dressed in dishevelled clothes, rocker-type person. Bands such as Zodiac Mindwarp and Pop Will Eat Itself were popular with grebo's. **UK**

greb, n.

gob of spittle and mucus snorted back from the nose and ejected. Used as 'I grebbed in Dave's parka hood!' *Circa* 1970s **UK (NW)**

greeny/gremlin/grolly, n.

something green and unpleasant you cough up – consists of phlegm and spit. As in 'urgh, he's coughed up a gremlin!' *Circa* 1983 onwards **UK**

grem, n.

used at the time of the 'great skateboard craze' to cast aspersions on the skill of a particular skateboarder. *Skateboard* magazine at the time quoted it as meaning 'a crappy little tosser.' Calling someone a grem at the time was usually the start of a punch up or at least furious bickering as to who was the most skilled *Circa* 1989-90 **UK**

greyhound, n.

mini skirt. So short it is very close to the hair **UK**

griffage, n.

'Low slung' trouser crotch. Term local to contributor's school named after a lad called 'Griffin' whose trouser crotch area always hung around his knees. This condition is usually caused by a trousers too big/no belt combo scenario. Griffage officially occurs when crutch area=greater than 4" from scrote. Usage: Shout 'GRIFFAGE!' whilst in the company of a friend in the know. Friend must then spot said griffage and point *Circa* 1980s **UK**

grifter, n.

model of bicycle made by Raleigh during the 1970s, midway between a Chopper and BMX in fashion chronology, but lacking the distinction of those two models. The Grifter line

(large to small) was: Grifter, Striker, Boxer *c.f.* Chopper, BMX
UK

grig, n.
used to describe an unpleasant, undesirable or unnecessary
substance, substances, object, or subject e.g. 'What is all this
GRIG on my windshield?', or 'Where is all this GRIG coming
from?', or even 'Get out! and take your GRIG with you!'
UK

grillopad, n.
(1) an excessively annoying or stupid person
(2) 'excessive' pubic hair on a female (usu.)
AUS

grimble, n.
game, similar to 'Scramble', but usually as a result of an accidental dropping of any article, either indoors or outdoors.
Property was nearly always kicked to destruction, causing
major problems if it was a school text or library book *f.* 1970s
UK (S)

grip/gripper, n.
(1) sideburns (or any facial/cheek hair that doesn't quite
form a beard). The term was a contraction of 'bugger-grips'
as they were something to hang on to while in the act. By definition, anyone who had sideburns then became a 'gripper'.
(2) in South Wales, also means an old person, usually male.
Probably to do with the way they're always gripping onto
handrails etc. with their bony knuckles, but also implies a
certain scariness, "like they're going come and 'grip' you if
you play football outside their house" **UK (SE), UK (Wal)**

grits, n.
undies. Used as 'oh she had on bigger grits than Bridget

107

Jones!' *Circa* 1990s **UK (W)**

grog, n./v.
(1) spittle, to spit e.g. 'I grogged on Mr Wertham's car.'
(2) alcohol
UK (Scot)

grot, n.
pornography. Used as 'Neil's got some grot in his locker. He's showing it at first break'. This use developed from 'grotty', itself a contraction of the word 'grotesque'.

grouse, n.
'really good' – similar in use to the way 'cool' is used today. Contributor particularly remembers seeing the following verse on a toilet wall, in among the usual 'Darryl is a wanker' type of graffitti:

'Be a man and not a mouse,
Pull your dick – it's fuckin' grouse!'

Still occasionally heard in adult conversation today **AUS**

grover, n./v.
the act of grabbing the genitals of a male counterpart and squeezing until the person writhed in pain. e.g. 'Bill gave me a grover/grovered me and it hurt like hell.' *Circa* 1980s
USA (Phil)

'growling at the badger', ph.
performing oral sex on a girl *Circa* 1973–78 **UK (NW)**

grovel, n.
playground scrummage whereby one child throws a fistful of

football cards, sweets or other playground collectables, unwanted by them or stolen off someone else, into the air whilst shouting 'GROVEL' at the top of their voices. Every other child in the playground would scramble around to try to grab the said free collectable. Originated, it is thought, in Liverpool. **UK (NE)**

grundy/'undie grundy', v.
for one or more assailants to seize waistband of selected victim's underpants and pull up same (sharply) to cause maximum pain and distress. A horrible craze which briefly swept the secondary schools of northwest Kent
c.f. wedgie *Circa* 1980–85 **UK (S)**

grundy, n.
old-fashioned, obselete i.e. 'look at that old grundy' or 'that's grundy' *Circa* 1980s **UK (SE)**

gub, n.
describes an unusually dense or gullible individual. A person who wallows in ignorance. Also Gubler, Gublord, Gubmeister General, Forrest Gub, Gubenator, Rub-a-Dub-Gub, Gubby Bear etc. etc. Contributor says foolish behaviour in a Chippenham pub may result in regular revivals *Circa* 1980s **UK (W)**

guff, v.
to break wind *c.f.* fart

gumping, v.
1) running about the playground, in no particular direction, as if you had your head stuck up your arse.
2) Also widely used in football. i.e for someone who makes a selfish, crap, head-down run up-field... oblivious to what's

going on around them! *f. Forrest Gump*-'Run Forest, Run'

gussie, n.
some sort of insult. Used as 'you gussie'. Generally used to imply inferiority, also has overtones of homosexuality. Used extensively in the North West of England (or at least in a small town called Ulverston) *Circa* 1980–85 **UK (NW)**

guts (dropped your ...), n.
break wind in a silent manner but with terrific aroma. The 'dropper' is usually proud of his work 'Watch out, I've dropped me guts' **UK**

gwli, n.
a narrow passage e.g. between blocks of toilets or buildings **UK (Wal)**

'gypsy (going for a...)', ph.
urinating. *f.* rhyming slang: (either) gypsy's kiss=piss (or) Gypsy (Rose) Lee=wee
UK (SE)

H

'haddaway and shite', ph.
if someone is annoying, or 'talking rubbish' used as 'Awh, haddaway and shite man'. It is a term from the dialect of Yorkshire (UK) which in fact means 'Please go away and defecate.' Has nothing to do with early 1990s singer Haddaway, famous only for that one-hit-wonder 'What is Love?'. **UK (NE)**

hairy eyeball, n.
hostile or dubious gaze. Used as 'That guy was giving us the hairy eyeball!' *Circa* current **UK**

ham, n.
someone (usu. boy) with no pubic hair. Used as 'You're a ham aren't you?' It was once used as an example of dialect in a top set English lesson, much to the amusement of the students! *Circa* 2000+ **UK (SE)**

hammock, n.
sanitary towel (term usu. used by males) *f.* 'hammock for a lazy cunt' *c.f.* jamrag **UK (Wal)**

hand jive, v.
masturbation. Used e.g. 'I was red route so I did the hand jive to stop him whining all night' Describes giving a guy a

'wank'. Taken from the movie *Grease* where they are all singing and dancing in the gym hall. The dance moves are all highly appropriate *Circa* 1980s **USA**

hand-job, v.
manually masturbate a male. Stimulate the penis by rubbing with the hand – usually to ejaculation. Used as 'I wasn't going down on him as I didn't know when he last washed it so I gave him a hand-job' *Circa* current **UK**

hand shandy/handy shandy, n.
masturbation *Circa* 1980s **UK**

'hand-to-gland combat', ph.
energetic masturbation session. **AUS**

hanging, n.
gross, disgusting. Usually used to describe a woman e.g. 'Did you see that? Face like a bag 'o' nails! She was really hanging!' *f.* practice of hanging game until high **UK (SE)**

harami, n.
apparently, harami means bastard in Urdu. Seems it's still used in India and Pakistan and is a very common slang word. Used as 'Man you know what? David is a harami!' In other words it is a substitute of 'bastard' *Circa* 1960s
UK (S)

hard, adj.
tough. To be considered 'hard' was the epitome of a wimpy schoolboy's schoolyard dreams. **UK**

headlights, n.
the sight of a girl's nipples erect and showing through her shirt, bikini top etc. Used as 'Wow – Mary's headlights were

beaming tonight! She was either just back from jogging or was really pleased to see me!' *c.f.* peanut smuggler *Circa* 2000 **CAN**

heave a Havana, v.
defecate. Going to the bathroom (Toilet humour)
Used to describe the feeling when you really are bursting for a crap or you've just had an almighty crap. Those times when you look at in the bowl and think 'FUCKIN' HELL! Did I just do that?' *Circa* 1990s **UK**

heez, n.
heez means bad, 'gay', stupid, or scuzzy. It is used in many different ways, such as 'that is heezed out to the maximum' or 'I'll give that an Awwwww Heez' or 'You're pretty heezy' **UK (NE)**

hella, adj.
extremely, greatly, super, a lot e.g. 'Your mom is hella hot!', 'He gets hella play!', 'That's hella cool.'**USA**

hellish/'ellish, adj.
used to describe something/someone which is excellent, great, wonderful. ie 'Darren has just got a Grifter bike. You should see it, it's ellish'. Was pronounced 'ellish in the contributor's neck of the woods. Hartlepudlians are great 'H' droppers. **UK (NE)**

hermit, n.
hermit means that you're somebody that sits in their house all day and wants to be alone. In a football match it can also mean somebody that never touchs the ball and just stands, usually a geeky boy *Circa* 2000 **UK (Scot.)**

hershey highway, n.
anal sex. Used in USA, where 'taking the Hershey Highway' carries the same meaning as 'fudge packing' or 'travelling up the Marmite motorway'. **USA**

high beam, adj.
used to describe nipples being erect, using the idea of high-beam lights being right up in your eyes.

Usefully used in conjunction with the word nipply (meaning cold). 'Look at Pamela Anderson, she's on high-beam. You can tell the air conditioning's a bit nipply!' *c.f.* headlights, peanut smuggler *Circa* 1970s+ **AUS**

himshe, n.
derogatory term for a male transsexual undergoing a sex change operation. Unfortunately, after breast implants and oestrogen ingestion, the hapless moron ran out of money and was forced to remain with breasts and facial hair *Circa* 1990s **UK (Wal.)**

hiney, n.
buttocks. An unusual word heard on US sitcoms but with an obscure derivation. One guess is that it is a corruption of the German word 'Hind' (similarly with the word 'hinterland')

hitler, n.
to wipe your finger through your ass crack, then wipe it on someone's top lip *c.f.* dirty sanchez *Circa* 1990s **UK**

'hitler has only got one ball...' song
Sung to the tune of Colonel Bogey's March:

> Hitler has only got one ball
> The other is in the Albert Hall
> His mother,

The dirty bugger
Cut it off when he was small
Hitler has only got one ball
Hess has both but they're small
Himmler had something similar
But poor old Goebbals
Had no balls at all…

Repeat, ad nauseum.

For some reason people were still singing this in the 1980s
Circa 1940s+ **UK (Wal.)**

'hit or miss (going for a…)', ph.

rhyming slang describing your intention of leaving the immediate vicinity in order to micturate. **UK (Scot)**

hock a loogey, v.

'hock a loogey'. Exactly the same as 'flob race', only known as loogy-hocking in the USA *c.f.* flob race **USA**

hojo mojo, n.

punishment consisting of the scraping of a knuckle hard against the scalp **UK (SE)**

hom, n.

(Pronounce as 'hhhhhhhhhhhhhhhhooooooooooooooommm-mmmmmmm'). A Homosexual (obviously), but … there's more! The key to 'hom' is pronunciation. 'You …. hhhhhh-hh—uuu— ahhhhhhhhhommmmmmmmmmmmmmmmmmmmm-mmmm' somewhere between a sharp intake of breath and a mantra, often lasting upwards of 20 seconds. Used as an insult *Circa* 1970-80s **UK (NW)**

hook/hawk, v.
vomit. As in 'he hooked his guts up'.

horse's hoof, n.
rhyming slang for homosexual. Horses hoof = poof *Circa* current **AUS. UK**

hopoate spike/hopoate (doing a...), n./v.
sliding a digit into someone's anus. *f.* John Hopoate was an Australian Rugby League player until March 2001 when he was caught onfield on camera ramming his thumb up an opponent's back passage. His defence for this was that it was a legitimate means of distracting the opponent, but after being roundly criticised on and off the field, and having become a total laughing stock, he decided to 'retire' from the game. **AUS**

horsey, n.
to play 'horsey' involved using a skipping rope as reins around a willing pupil's neck then basically running around like a horse and master (not as kinky and more fun than it sounds when you're 8 years old).

Also used for riding a child on your back (also called piggyback) or dangling a child on your knee. Lately referred to as a term for molesting children (i.e. straddling a youngster on your knee and bouncing them up and down).
UK (Mid), USA

hoy, v.
to throw. Currently usage includes alcohol induced vomiting e.g. 'I was so pissed last night, I hoyed like a squealy pig when I got home.' **UK (NE)**

howfer, n.

an ugly girl or woman *f.* abbreviation of 'How ferking ugly is she?' *Circa* 1980s **UK (Scot)**

hughie, v.

onomatopoeic word for the forcible ejection of vomit, for example whilst driving the porcelain bus. Popularised by the brilliant Welsh comic Max Boyce *c.f.* five finger spread, spew *Circa* 1970s+ **UK (Wal)**

humungous

not just big… the biggest, used as in 'Mr Jones had a huuu-munnnnggous bogey hanging out of his nose in Maths!'

hundred, n.

test of hardness which involved another person pinching the back of your hand at a specified percentage. The hundred was the ultimate, which was precisely as hard as the pincher could manage. The level of pain inflicted depended on the strength of the pincher and their fingernails; flesh removal was not uncommon *c.f.* beano *Circa* 1980-84

I

IDGAD, ph.
acronym for 'I don't give a damn'. In response to someone saying something entirely trivial, uninteresting or completely irrelevant. Idgad is the abbreviated form of 'fmdidgad', pronounced 'fumd-idgad'. This in turn is an abbreviation of the line from *Gone with the Wind*, namely, 'Frankly my dear, I don't give a damn'. Often this line is only partially abbreviated, so delivered, 'Frankly my dear... idgad' *Circa* 1990s **UK**

IDST, ph.
IDST is an abbreviation for 'If Destroyed Still True'. This is written after a piece of defamatory graffiti e.g. 'Mark is a fat jabba IDST' to tell everyone that the statement is a true one. Variations include INDST – If Not Destroyed Still True. Contributor not sure when this first appeared but it was known when he was at school and he still sees it on walls today *Circa* 1980s+ **UK**

illywhacker, n.
trickster, someone not to be trusted. **AUS**

'I'm rubber and you're glue...', rh.
when someone calls you names, you respond by reciting in an infuriating sing-song manner:

I'm rubber and you're glue,
Whatever you say,
Bounces off me
And sticks to you!'

Pretty much universal – this was sent in from Malaysia, where English is the second language to many, yet this rhyme has widespread use *Circa* 1990s **UK, MALAYSIA**

injectified, n.
only cure for the lurgi. Persons being given the lurgi would then have to run after other persons and try to touch them and shout 'lurgi', then pretend to inject their arm, and shout 'injectified', so that that person could not transmit the lurgi back to them. Unfortunately it wore off after a while, and people who smelled developed extremely strong strains of the lurgi, which couldn't be combated by injectifying *c.f.* lurgi *Circa* 1980s **UK (SE)**

'ip dip dog shit...', rh.
when working out who was 'it' for a game, you'd all put your left foot in a circle, and then one of you would say 'ip dip dog shit you are not on it.' whilst touching each foot in turn, Accepted method of choosing who was it *Circa* 1978. **UK**

irish waterfall, n.
cigarette smoking technique, usually practiced by girls, whereby the smoke is taken into the mouth and then inhaled up through the nose. Also known as a 'french inhale' *Circa* current **UK**

itchy beard/itchy boris/itchy/itchoy, n.
expression indicating disbelief. Itchy beard can also be

accompanied by the hand motion of stroking an invisible goaty beard on your chin with your fingertips *c.f.* chinny reck-on, Tutankhamun **UK**

J

jaar, n.
accompanied by a rubbing of the chin, it was used to indicate that someone was being a little 'liberal with the truth.' Normally followed by the person's name which typically ended in ' – eh' e.g 'Jaaar harr-eh' *c.f.* chinny reck-on, **UK (ME)**

jab, n.
similar in form and effect to 'clogsies' and 'injectified' but added a dimension whereby one could shout 'Jab for life' which indicated that the involved party could not be tagged for the rest of the ad-hoc game *Circa* 1970s

jabba, n.
insult, especially used towards anyone considered tubby or somewhat less than sexually desirable. Used as 'You fat Jabba', or 'He/She's a fat Jabba', or 'Hey Jabba!'

The third Star Wars film introduced a new word into playground slang; all large kids henceforth being compared to the slug-like alien of the opening sequence, Jabba the Hut. Very rarely used without being preceded by the adjective 'fat', though in Australia it is often used as 'Jabba the Slut' *Circa* 1990s **UK**

jack, v.
to steal. To 'jack' something e.g. 'Hey. Someone jacked my calculator!', 'Chelsea tried to jack my pen, that bitch' *Circa* 2000 **UK, USA (W)**

'jack the biscuit', ph.
something really good. Used as 'I feel like Jack the biscuit in my new trainers.' *Circa* 1990s **UK**

jackanory, n.
whenever someone at school would start telling something that was clearly a made-up story (or seriously exaggerated), it was the duty of those listening to start chanting *Jackanory* in order to humiliate the story-teller. Jackanory was the name of a BBC TV story-telling programme *Circa* 1980s **UK (SE)**

jaffa, n.
(1) person with 'seedless' sperm i.e. 'firing blanks', having 'no lead in their pencil' – used by David Jason as Derek Trotter, aka 'Del Boy', in the TV series *Only Fools and Horses*. (2) a person with enormous bollocks. **UK**

jacky-jumper, n.
a string of small explosive fireworks created by packing a small amount of gunpowder into a long tube of brown paper along with a thin fuse. The paper is then 'pinched' and folded such that it looks something like a series of attached z's.

When the fuse is lit the first part explodes sending the firework in an unpredictable direction. The fuse continues to burn, exploding each section in turn. Throwing a lit jacky-jumper into a crowd of kids was a good laugh... unless they (or an adult) caught you *c.f.* banger **UK (Wal)**

jake, n.
poor person, smelly, wears Oxfam clothing. Contributor said

he had a 'jake' in primary school. His name was Frank and he smelled of piss *Circa* 1980s **UK (Scot.)**

jamboree bag, n.
inexpensive pre-packed bag of sweets of various kinds – often included a toy or 'charm' *c.f.* lucky–bag **UK**

jammy, n.
to have great luck, An expression of disbelief to someone else's good luck. Tended to be accompanied by a slight insult e.g. 'You jammy get' (get=git)

jamrag, n.
sanitary towels (term usu. used by males) *c.f.* hammock **UK**

janky, adj.
something dysfunctional, old or substandard *Circa* 1990s–00s **USA**

jap's eye, n.
the exit of the urethra, otherwise known as that little hole you pee through (if you're a bloke) *Circa* 1980s **UK (Wal)**

japanese burn, n.
like a chinese burn but round your neck *c.f.* chinese burn

jarred (well...),v.
a 'put down'. Used on someone who had been put right, or in some way disappointed or distressed, usually prefixed by 'well'. e.g. 'I bet you were well jarred when Mr Nobbs con fiscated your Invader 1000.' Origins unknown*Circa* 1984-87 **UK**

jasper, n.
a wasp or bee (origin unknown)

jawbreakers, n.

these were enormous gobstoppers with different coloured (and flavoured) layers. We all flirted daily with the real danger of horrible suffocation from these huge sweets – these days there'd be a pressure group lobbying Parliament.

Great excitement was caused by the advent of the 'red hot' jawbreaker (which caused mild chemical burns to the roof of your mouth) *Circa* 1980s **UK**

jesus boots/jesus creepers n.

flat soled sandals, (the sole is similar to that of the 'brothel creeper' but with a thinner profile) *c.f.* MGBs *Circa* 1970s–80s **UK (SE)**

jibs, n.

(1) describe something that someone does not want to say e.g. a coarse word such as sex or fingering someone
(2) as a word to replace any other word really. An example: 'Did you see that man jibbing along?' There are many different forms of the word jibs, including, jibbed, jibbing, jib and jibbified and all of these words are in extensive use in many secondary schools in SE England *Circa* 1990s **UK (SE)**

jigger, n.

in Tottenham, North London, a jigger was a homemade go-kart constructed from a scaffold plank, a set of 'class' pram wheels, a big bolt and rope (for steering) e.g. 'Wanna help me build a jigger?' *Circa* 1965 **UK (SE)**

Jim (An accident happened to my brother...), poem

A contributor heard this back in his childhood:

An accident happened to my brother Jim
When somebody threw a tomato at him

Tomatoes are juicy and don't bruise the skin,
But this one was specially packed in a tin!

UK

jimmy hat, n.
condom. One might say 'Hey man, let me borrow a jimmy hat, so I can go smash?' *Circa* 1990s **USA**

Jimmy Hill/jimmy, n.
expression indicating disbelief. The associated 'action' was stroking the chin in reference to the somewhat abnormally sized chin possessed by said 'Jimmy'.
c.f. chinny reck-on, itchy beard, Tutankhamun **UK**

jimmy tap, v.
to strike at the male genitals, usually with an object rather than a fist (e.g. 'he took off his watch and gave me a jimmy tap') *Circa* 2000 **UK**

jinx!, exc.
when 2 people say the same word at the same time, you had to be the first to shout 'jinx!' so that the other person couldn't speak. If 'jinx' was said at the same time then you had to be first to say 'Double jinx'.

jobbey/jobbie, n.
excrement, poo, shit, turds etc. A word much favoured by comedian Billy Connolly *Circa* 1970s-to date
UK (Scot)

jobbey-jabber/jobbie-jabber, n.
homosexual. A very thinly veiled reference to anal sex. Widely used in Northern Scotland, but also noted in other areas. It is likely that it came into widespread use as the word

'jobby' became popularised (as Jobbie) by Billy Connolly in the 70s *Circa* 1970s–to date **UK (Scot)**

joey, n.

derog. An excessively stupid or unpleasant person. One contributor supplied the following entered verbatim:

'To infer that the recipient was, in some manner, mentally impaired or stupid. In widespread use (in my experience) throughout London schools in the early 1980s. Derives from Joey Deacon, an unfortunate, severely mentally handicapped man featured on children's TV show *Blue Peter*. Or rather, thrown in front of a camera crew & routinely patronized once a week by Simon Groom and his lover, that platinum quadruped Goldie. Originally intended to improve children's understanding of the plight of the disabled. Failed.'

c.f. spack *Circa* 1980s **UK (SE)**

joey, n.

condom *Circa* late 1970s **NZ**

johnny clegg, n.

See entry for wedgie. **UK**

johnny no-stars, n.

a young man of substandard intelligence, the typical adolescent who works in a burger restaurant. The 'no-stars' comes from the badges displaying stars that staff at fast-food restaurants often wear to show their level of training. **USA**

johnny (rubber...), n.

condom. In the age of the 'Sex Pistols' this gave rise to the following 'joke'. One punk music lover to another 'Is this Johnny Rotten?', 'Nah ... shouldn't be... I only bought it the other day' *Circa* late 1970s **UK**

jonah, n.
used to describe an unpopular person with no friends. As in 'See smelly Joe over there on his own, what a Jonah', 'piss-off Terry, you Jonah!' This use probably linked to the biblical story of 'Jonah and the Whale'. Jonah spent a considerable amount of time on his own in a whale's belly, so he was probably quite smelly! *Circa* 1980 **UK**

jubbly/jubblie/jubilee, n.
confection (usually purchased from ice cream van) consisting of frozen TipTop fruit drink in plastic container *f.* Jubbly (trade name of orange drink in triangular wax cartons **UK**

jugular japeries, n.
breasts. Used as 'Ooooh she's got a nice pair of jugular japeries!' *Circa* 2002 **UK**

jungle juice, n.
liquid from wet beef curtains *c.f.* beef curtains **UK**

jungle treatment, n.
at primary school, start of summer, a random kid would be held down on the school field, and asked by the much stronger protagonist 'Do you get hayfever?', presenting the kid with a dilemma: if he says 'No', a reply of 'You won't mind me doing this then' will be given, and mounds of grass will be stuffed in his face and down shirt. If he replies in the affirmative, however, he subjects himself to an identical fate. As an added bonus, your shirt would be covered in grass stains and you could later expect a bollocking from your mum *Circa* 1980s **UK**

junk, n.
male genitalia *Circa* 1990s **USA, UK**

jupve, n.
foul-smelling individual with mentally subnormal tendencies often less well off financially than their tormentors. Derived from a special needs GCSE equivalency course which involved the hapless participants riding around the playground on rusted motorcycles with ludicrously big helmets often giving the rider's head an egg-like appearance. Also jutte, jupveous and jup. Still often heard in drinking establishments *Circa* 1989-94 **UK (Mid)**

K

'Kangaroos loose in the top paddock (Got a few...)' ph.
mentally ambiguous. Prone to saying/doing strange things *Circa* current **AUS**

kappa, n.
Either a handicapped person or an excessively stupid or unpleasant person *f.* handicap(per) *c.f.* spack, mentler, joey, flid **UK (NW)**

kappa slappa, n.
someone who wears Kappa clothes all the time *f.* Kappa. Trade name for range of 'outdoor clothing' and 'sportswear' **UK (Scot)**

kecks, n.
(1) trousers
(2) underpants
AUS, UK

keener, n.
boot-licker, brown-noser, suck-up, or sycophant **CAN**

keep dog, n.
keep lookout, guard dog. When a group realise an unfore-

seen opportunity of theft and there is sufficient reason to believe the proprietor, a teacher or dinner lady is nearby, the lesser-experienced member is nominated to 'keep dog'. Unfortunately inexperience is highlighted in the breakdown of communication between keep dog and the perpetrators. Normally ending in a panicked getaway. Often dog is caught, being the last person leaving the scene. This is due to inexperience and holding the responsibility to inform every member as danger nears *Circa* 1980s **UK**

keggy, n.
large bruise or lump on head. Usually discoloured and/or painful.

keg-legs, n.
unkind name shouted at girls with 'fat' thighs or (more especially) calves *c.f.* cankle *Circa* 1960s **UK**

ket/ketts, n.
sweets. Any confectionary product certain to give you advanced tooth decay. Used as 'Here man, give us one of ya ketts!' Sweet (kett) as in cola cubes, midget gems, fruit pastilles etc. Origin unknown *Circa* 1980s **UK (NE)**

kevin/kev, n.
male of a low socio-economic class with reluctant facial hair who drives a Ford Escort, has an underage girlfriend, and wears lots of sports gear. More specific than a ned, they would take their cars to local parks to practice handbreak turns etc *Circa* 1980s *c.f.* ned, Sharon **UK (Mid)**

keys, n.
a 'shout'. Conveyed temporary immunity during certain games. Usually accompanied by a thumbs up sign.
UK (Scot)

kidney jab, n.
hand digs to the kidney area inflicted by several assailants upon a helpless victim. **UK (S)**

kier (pron. Chi-Err), n.
derog. term for a pupil of 'gypsy' descent. Note: spelling may be incorrect **UK (NE)**

kinder surprise, n.
describes a female who is 'top' heavy. e.g. big breasts, big waist, big hips and thighs...and skinny legs *c.f.* keg-legs
UK

kinnel, n.
exclamation of amazement *f.* FUCKING HELL

kipper, n.
vagina. Contributor can only remember using it up to about the age of 9 after which other words were discovered *Circa* 1983 **UK (NE)**

kirk, n.
person who has been circumcised *c.f.* zebbled

kissing teeth, v.
term given when you make that sucking/kissing sound against your teeth when you're pissed off at something. Maybe it's a Sarf Lahndon thing. This was popularised over the last 10 years by Jerry Seinfeld's habit of doing it on his TV show.

klingon, n.
(1) piece of excrement that sticks stubbornly to the buttock and/or buttock hairs.
(2) an excessively stupid or unpleasant person

(3) a small child, brother/sister/babysittee, who insists on following you round the whole time, preferably being held or carried, or 'clings-on' to your leg

knacker, n./v.
(1) unwashed thieving person, often said to be found living in caravans on lay-bys on B-roads in Britain *c.f.* gippo
(2) to destroy e.g. 'One good kick and I knackered that good and proper.'
(3) to tire e.g. 'I just walked 10 miles home. I'm knackered!'
UK

knickers, n.
underpants, usu. those worn by females. 'Getting into a girl's knickers' is a favourite pastime for adolescent boys **UK**

knob-jockey, n.
Literally 'a professional rider of knobs'. Can either be used to insult a promiscuous girl, or a homosexual man (although the latter is more common)

knob-scratch, n.
someone who annoys you or bugs you constantly. Used as 'Oi knob-scratch piss off!' **UK (Mid)**

knock up, v.
to impregnate a female – usually out of wedlock. Also referred to as being 'in the club', having 'a bun in the oven', etc. **USA**

'knock your block off', ph.
threat. Signal with intent to decapitate someone by striking them so hard their head will be removed from physical contact with their body *c.f.* block **UK (NW)**

knuckle duster, n.
the knuckle duster is a weapon used for fighting. Often made of brass, these things were worn on the hand so that when the fist was clenched they strengthened and protected the knuckles when a fist blow was struck. They are/were often carried around in the pocket and 'decorated' with extras such as sharp stars or possibly a knife blade, all of which were directed towards making the wound inflicted as serious as possible *Circa* 1950s onwards **UK**

knuckle sandwich, n.
a punch in the mouth **UK**

knuckle shuffle, n.
male masturbation **UK**

L

ladgefull, adj.
'Oh my god you're so ladgefull' – Embarrassing, shameful. Even worse than when your mum gets her hankie out, spits on it and wipes your face in front of all your mates. Also may be shortened to ladge: 'That's soooo ladge' *Circa* 1980-84 **UK (Mid)**

ladgin, adj.
used to describe something quite unfashionable i.e. 'Those shoes are ladgin!' and 'he's really ladgin'. Ginger people were often referred to as Ladginners. Got quite trendy in usage – so much so that when the contributor was in the first year, the fifth years opened a tuck shop called LadginChow *f*. Origin unknown, but it has a faint 'chinese' air about it *Circa* 1990s **UK**

la/lah, n.
mate, friend e.g. 'Alright la?', 'Got a spare fag la?'. One possibility sent in was that Liverpudlians used it cos they could never be arsed pronouncing words correctly and it actually means 'lad' (boy) *f*. 'lah' could be a diminutive of 'love' or 'lad' (see above). **UK (NW), Sing.**

lamp, v.
hit e.g. 'He lamped me a treat after I slagged off his bint!'
UK (Wal)

'lard the rails', ph.
run urgently, often away from some imminent threat.
Usually, this cry was heard in the midst of dubious activity,
(often from a lookout) in the event of being caught. The term,
I'm told, derived from the rather curious epidemic of Urban
Aggressive Street Manoeuvring, which first began around
1994-5.

The idea was that, if lacking a skateboard, punters could
use their feet to negotiate tricky obstacles (ramps, poles,
benches, etc) in a stylish way. When attempting railslides in
this way, it was common knowledge that rubbing a little pig
fat on the appropriate rail would make the trick much faster,
and more impressive overall. So, for a speedy getaway, lard
the rails *Circa* 1990s **UK**

lash, n.
out raging, a wild night out drinking and chasing totty e.g.
'out on the lash' **UK**

leak (taking a ...), v.
urinating **UK**

'leg it!', v.
action of running away, or an instruction to remove oneself
from a location with alacrity – for example after smashing
someone's window with a ball *Circa* 1973 – to date **UK**

leper, n.
general insult. Usually in relation to a lack of intelligence/
ability – after someone drops a bollock 'Christ – you really
screwed that up! What a leper!' **UK**

'less it!', ph.
cease, desist the action you are performing. e.g. 'Less It will yer!' (i.e. Please stop performing that action. It is annoying me immensely) *Circa* 1975+ **UK (NE)**

letch (to...), v.
to ogle in a lascivious manner **UK (S)**

lewinsky (getting a ...), n.
receiving oral sex *f.* the saga of 'Monica and Bill' where the whole issue of what constitutes sexual contact was redefined *Circa* 1998 **UK (W)**

licky geed/grebe, n.
one with greasy hair **UK (S)**

lidder, n.
an idiot, someone clumsy *c.f.* flid. **UK (Mid)**

ling, v.
to throw or chuck. Implies throwing very hard, normally with intent to break something or hurt someone. **UK (SE)**

loafer, n.
someone who is large, either tall, fat, or both. Someone very clumsy, often falling over, or breaking things. Also referred to as a 'lumberer'. Used as 'Whoa, check out that great loafer!' *Circa* 1980s **UK (Wal)**

lobs, exc.
call when teacher was coming e.g. Keep lobs, stand lookout while others engage in fighting/burglary/sabotage etc. **AUS**

locked, v.
describes someone very drunk. Used as 'He's locked' from

'locked out of his head', 'locked out of my tree *Circa* 1990s
UK (SW)

logued, v.

'He went mental and Logued at Mr Jones' A contributor
writes "A lad called Phillip Logue was reprimanded by our
PE teacher once and was asked to wait in the PE office (which
was obviously considered a hotbed of gay activity) for a bollocking. To which he responded 'Why sir, are you going to do
me up the arse?'

The most interesting thing was the pissed-off way he said
it, as if this was going to be his 1,000th anal intrusion by a PE
teacher. From thenceforth, any forthright riposte beyond normal bravery was known as a Logue" *Circa* 1986–87 **UK (SE)**

lollygagger, n.

lazy person. Someone who wanders around aimlessly **USA**

lollypopping, v.

hanging out with your friends and joking around *Circa* current **USA**

loopy, adj.

crazy. When used to describe a person, often accompanied by
twirling a finger pointed to the temple of the user in a loop-
ing motion and (if necessary) pushing the tongue down
between the bottom teeth and the chin.
UK

loosie/lucy, n.

single cigarettes sold by shopkeepers to schoolchildren (and
presumably to anyone else who couldn't afford £1.50 for a
pack of Embassy). Normally kept in a jar or glass on the shelf
by the ciggies. These were sold in blatant disregard of the law
prohibiting the sale of cigs to the under-16s. **UK (I. of Man)**

losty, n.

insane. Someone who has 'lost the plot' – has erratic ideas and tries to put them into practice. Used most commonly by kids between the ages of 13 and 17 *Circa* 1999+ **AUS**

louis, n.

used as 'want to buy a louis?' Refers to a sixteenth of an ounce of hashish, which has always been a popular drug in UK playgrounds. After Louis XVI (sixteenth) **UK**

love bite, n.

small red bruise on the skin surface (usually neck area) caused by 'sucking' on the surface, i.e. creating a vacuum that breaks some blood vessels creating the distinctive markings. The name is due in part to a person showing a level of affection by allowing it to be done as it can be a painful process, and in part due to a belief that the bites are a normal part of lovemaking.

Girls who have them are viewed by guys with interest 'just in case they spontaneously become tarts'! Boys that have them are often sad case losers who have created them themselves by pinching and manipulating the skin to give the impression they have a girlfriend *Circa* 1950s+ **UK**

love-monkey, n.

someone who, despite being excessively hairy, is found attractive by another *Circa* 1990s **USA**

lucky-bag, n.

a small paper bag containing a selection of sweets and often containing a small toy as well *c.f.* Ten-Pence-Mix

lugs, n.

ears (used in context: 'I'll batt yer lugs for yer') *c.f.* wingnut

lunchbag, n.
a loser, person with no friends, doesn't 'fit in' and does nothing right *f.* people who brought lunch to school in a bag, then went off to sit and eat it alone because no one liked them. **UK**

lunch-box (open the ...), n.
fart **AUS**

lung butter, n.
phlegm. e.g. 'That was some tasty lung butter!', or 'I just coughed up a big hunk of lung butter' – referring to the phlegm coughed up due to illness *Circa* 1990s – to date **USA**

lurgi/lurgy, n.
imaginary sickness that 1) girls had and you contracted by kissing them, or 2) you had as a matter of course from being smelly or dirty or not being like the other kids

The imaginary disease of the lurgi could also be spontaneously developed by someone in order to start a game whereby the afflicted child had to pass it on to someone else by touch. Other children could protect themselves by calling 'injected!' and miming using a syringe in their arm.

The word actually originates from an episode of the British 50s radio programme *The Goon Show*. The episode was called 'Lurgi Strikes Britain', telling the story of an epidemic of the fictitious disease – and 45 years later the word is used universally across British schools by children who have never heard of The Goons *c.f.* injectified, cooties *Circa* 1950s onwards **UK**

lush, adj.
very good, tasting really nice, looking really attractive. i.e. 'She's really lush', 'That tastes lush', 'Did you see that pro-

gramme last night, it was lush' *f.* luscious *Circa* early/mid 1980s **UK**

lush mcgush, adj.
superlative of lush. If it wasn't just lush, but particularly good, it was Lush McGush.
c.f. lush *Circa* 1970 – 80s **UK (SM)**

luzz, v.
to chuck or throw **UK (SE)**

M

macca, adj.
enormous, huge *f.* massive, mega *c.f.* humungous.
UK (SE)

macho test (the...), n.
a test of one's machismo conducted by rubbing at the fore-arm with an eraser until the skin is rubbed raw. Called a 'macho test' it was really more a test of one's stupidity. What basically happened was one would take those pink school erasers, or the eraser from a pencil, and rub the forearm vig-orously until multiple layers of skin and forearm hair were removed, leaving the area bald, shiny, and very, very, very raw. The fact that one could do this to themselves and endure it was supposed to be a testament to their machismo *Circa* 1981-83 **USA**

macknah, exc.
an expression of disinterest *f.* an imitation of a noise made by the computer game PACMAN when a ghost is devoured *c.f.* biggins **UK (SE)**

magno-knads, n.
one who has testicles of magic property or great strength *Circa* 2000 **UK**

mallie, n.
homosexual. Used as term of abuse to describe somebody who was gay (or appeared to be). Also used to describe the act of homosexual intercourse (i.e. 'He mallied him!') *f.* Allegedly, the word came into use following an incident with a boy named 'Malcolm' and another man, but this may be apocryphal. **UK (NE)**

mallet, n.
person discovered by his peers, in changing rooms and similar, to be without pubic hair. Used as 'He's a mallet!' or 'You're a mallet!' *c.f.* ham **UK**

malco, n.
a person who has a lack of co-ordination. An abbrev. of malco-ordinated. Handy for shouting at goalkeepers who have two left hands and are all thumbs *Circa* 1990s **UK**

manimal, n.
taken from the early 80s TV show of the same name, about a private detective who could change into various animals at will (accompanied with an extreme close up of a pulsating hand). This game involved clenching a fist and then wiggling the knuckles and tendons whilst going 'I'm Manimal!' *Circa* 1983–84 **UK (S)**

manky, adj.
describes something revolting or gross. From the French 'manque' *Circa* 1950s+ **UK (Wal)**

manners, n.
'manners' was a term used to point out that another kid was inferior to you, in the way they dressed, at sports, physically, or just in general. If you were 'under manners' this could also mean that you were in trouble, or being watched by a teacher

in class, so had to be quiet. Obviously, it was used to tease and show that you could still continue to behave badly, whilst they were – indeed – 'under manners' *Circa* 1880–84 **UK (SE)**

man-of-atlantis, n.
useless swimming stroke based on Patrick Duffy in the television series.

map-o'-tassie, n.
women's pubic hair. Due to a strange quirk of fate, the island of Tasmania looks exactly the same shape as the area of a woman's untrimmed pubic hair. **AUS**

maremare, n.
corruption of Nightmare. Said to someone that is not doing something correctly or is having bad luck i.e. 'you are having a maremare, mate!' **UK (SE)**

marbles, n.
game in many varieties but in its most basic form, normally involves the striking of one spherical glass object with another **UK (NE)**

mard/mardy, n./adj.
moody, sulky, stroppy or in a tantrum. Used as in 'Having a mard', 'He's mardy', 'He's a mard', 'Mardy bastard.' If you piss someone off and they are upset, you say 'Mmm... mmmmm... mmmmmm... MMMMaaaaaaaaaaaaaarrrrddddd' in a high-pitched voice, causing them to go red in the face and boil with rage, hence even more mardy than they were before *Circa* 1980s **UK (NW, Mid)**

marmite driller/miner, n.
offensive term for homosexual male *f*. Marmite – thick brown

yeast extract spread on toast and the like in the UK.
UK (Mid)

marmite motorway, n.
anal passage.

mash up, v.
drunk as a skunk. Smashed out of the head. Pissed *Circa* 1990s **UK (SE)**

mattress man, n.
term denoting a particularly egregious form of wanker. This, quoted verbatim, is a fine illustration: "At school during the summer they would leave the fire exit door at the end of the dining hall open for ventilation. Through it you could see the fire escape for one of the boarding houses. This house (North 'A') was traditionally known for its sexual deviancy (e.g. amongst its members it was prized to be invited to join the Ginger Pubes Club).

One summer evening during the second sitting of dinner a commotion was caused as large numbers of diners were congregating by the door in awful fascination at the sight on the North 'A' fire escape. The 'Mattress Man', having eaten in the first sitting had retired to the fire escape for a quick one off the wrist. In the throes of passion he chanced upon a discarded mattress leaning against the wall in the fire escape and vented his passions upon it fairly vigorously. Quite apart from half the school witnessing this so did most of the teachers who had to come over to see what was causing the commotion in the dining hall. Subsequently even they called him Mattress Man. Needless to say he left the school soon after." *Circa* 1988 **UK (SE)**

maw (yer...), n.
pronounced, 'yer-maw' as in 'claw', this is a classic riposte

144

when one's string of stand-by retorts has been exhausted. The always effective 'thing to say when there is nothing else to say' and in that way it is very much the supercalifragilis-ticexpealidocious of the scruffy playground. When stuck for a witty rejoinder merely resort to 'Oh aye...yer maw'. Eternal argument winner. Is often countered with subsequent elabo-rations 'Aye...your maw'; 'Yer fuckin' maw'; and the endless-ly creative and enigmatic 'Aye... yer maw's baws!'
(Ed: for the unenlightened, maw = mother, baw = balls)
c.f. baw heid **UK**

meat and two veg, n.
male genitalia *c.f.* wedding tackle, family jewels **UK**

meaty, n.
material ejected from the mouth consisting of a mixture of saliva and mucus, that contains a high proportion of mucus. In other words, spit with a fair amount of snot in it e.g. 'I did a meaty on that prefect' *c.f.* semi-phlegmy, gob, snot
Circa 1970s–80s **UK**

meesh, n.
'standing on street corners drinking cider' type of person who goes looking for a fight every 2 minutes as he thinks he's well hard, whereas in fact, he's a skinny, scummy little runt. A Meesh will usually be found in South Wales
c.f. scally *Circa* 1990s **UK (Wal)**

meff/meffer, n.
(1) dirty, smelly individual, or a person with disgusting habits
(2) a vagrant.
f. possibly a derivative of 'methylated', as in the spirits, the tramp's drink of choice *Circa* 1960s+ **UK**

mega, adj.

overused word that meant almost anything 'good' or 'great'. Can be used alone or with other words *Circa* 1980s **UK**

meh!, exc.

general exclamation. Tone of voice denotes meaning. Can be angry, overjoyed, confused, etc. Pronunciation as 'H' is highly aspirated, and the 'e' is pronounced like the 'e' is 'head' *Circa* 1990s **UK**

mekon, adj.

person with remarkably high forehead, bald person *f.* character in Dan Dare cartoon series, *Eagle Comic c.f.* Tefal, slaphead, spam head *Circa* 1950s+

mello, v.

"is where you push so hard to fart that you shit your pants" *Circa* current **UK**

melons/jugs/knobs/honkers, n.

female breasts. From an American perspective, these are all slang words used in describing women's breasts. 'Honkers' is not as common, but is used to describe breasts by the way they might be handled by a person... to be 'honked' like a circus clown's horn *Circa* 1950s+ **USA**

melvin, n

wedgie. Or a reverse-wedgie, i.e. pulling the frontside of someone's underwear as high as possible, or until he screams and cries in pain. Usually given to wiseass kids who taunt older classmates. Can be especially painful if the Melvin-receiver is wearing boxer shorts.

However, one contributor objected to the 'wedgie' definition and sent in the following:

'In my school this described the action of grabbing someone's testicles and twisting (especially when performed by a girl to get revenge over some form of sexual harassment). One girl, Kim, a couple of years above the contributor, was notorious for giving them, although he personally found her to be a very nice person. Used as "Watch out fer that Kim, she'll melvin yer!"' **USA, UK**

menner, n.
someone who is mentally or physically deficient. Note the fact that the local mental hospital (Silveroyds) was situated in the Leeds suburb of Menston, hence 'Menner', someone who came from Menston. But could also come from an abbreviation of 'mental' *c.f.* joey, mong, spac *Circa* 1960s–70s **UK (Mid)**

ment, n.
abbreviated from 'Mental'. Used to describe someone who seems unco-ordinated or performs an unco-ordinated act. For example, 'He missed the ball, the fat ment!' *Circa* 1990s **UK**

mental, adj.
can mean a whole range of things, such as mad, insane, stupid, brilliant, marvellous, bizarre, strange, extremely painful (of BMX accidents), loud or violent.

mentalist, n.
someone considered to be a bit lacking in the brain department: i.e. 'the lights are on but no one's home.' Always more effective when used as part of the phrase, 'You big spastic, you're a mentalist.' **UK**

mentler, n.
a mental person *c.f.* mental, mentalist, spack, nutjob, joey, flid, mong, eppy, div, bell-end

merf, n.
cowshit *Circa* 2000 **UK**

metal mouth, n.
unkind name for someone wearing braces on their teeth *c.f.* tin-grin, brace-face **USA**

metgod, n.
(pron. met-hod): a phrase used in celebration of a goal in a footy game in the schoolyard. Named after striker Johnny Metgod from the Dutch World Cup team. He became known for piledriving shots from about 30 yards, so any goal scored from distance would be followed by the scorer saying 'Metgod' in a pre-pubescent Motson-like-high-pitched-excited-voice, thus cracking windows nearby. Johnny played for a long period during the 1980s for Nottingham Forest, which indicates that this saying originated from that area.
UK (Mid)

MGBs, n.
alternative name for 'Jesus Boots', i.e. MGB = Moses Getaway Boots *c.f.* Jesus Boots **USA**

miff, n.
female genitalia or pubic hair. Used as 'D'yer gerrany miff in that film?', or 'Ey, I can see 'er miff!' *c.f.* muff *Circa* 1970-80s **UK (NW)**

MILF, n.
acronym which stands for 'Mother I'd Love to Fuck'. It is an adjective used by males, describing a mother of a friend that is hot, and you wouldn't mind fucking her. Can also be interchanged with DILF and GILF – daddies and grannies. MILF was used in the movie *American Pie* which is where the word has spread from *Circa* 1999 **USA**

millennium domes, n.

breasts. Contents of a Wonderbra, i.e. like the dome, extremely impressive when viewed from the outside, but actually
fuck-all in there worth seeing. **UK**

'milk, milk...', poem

relates to an anatomical description of the female form:

> Milk, milk,
> Lemonade,
> Turn the corner,
> Chocolate's made.

Circa 1970 **UK (SE)**

minda, n.

mentally challenged. When someone acts stupidly or is slow
on the uptake. Say, 'You minda!' ('i' as in 'rib', stress the first
syllable) and act as for 'durbrain'. Comes from Minda
Incorporated, the South Australian company which supports
people with intellectual disabilities *c.f.* dur-brain *Circa*
1980s–date **AUS**

minge, n.

female genital area, occasionally pubic hair only *c.f.* ginger-
minge **UK**

mingey, adj.

tightfisted, mean **UK**

mingin(g), adj.

(1) smelly, disgusting, ugly, horrid, putrid, gross
(2) ugly: often applied to a swamp donkey *c.f.* swamp donkey

(3) extremely drunk
Circa 1970s **UK**

ming-ray/ming-rayed, v.

an individual is 'ming-rayed' when his/her school-bag/fold-er is left unattended. Once noticed by someone, they alert others to join him, before instigating the act of 'ming-ray'; whereby the contents of the bag are emptied and spread as far as possible within the general vicinity before the victim notices/moves to prevent it. When the victim does notice, the word 'ming-ray' is shouted by the attackers, with prolonged emphasis on the 'ray' *Circa* 1990s
UK (SE)

mink, n.

describing someone who is disgusting or dirty. i.e. 'Quit pick-ing yer nose, Mink!' or 'He's a Fort William Mink!'. Mostly used north of the border, (Scotland) but understood if used with enough venom anywhere. Probably comes from either 'MINKY' brand cleaning cloths or 'Tink' being a tinker or tramp. Should also be noted that if you are a mink you can be described as a 'Minker', or as being 'Minkey' *c.f.* manky *Circa* 1970s **UK (Scot)**

mint/mintox/mont, adj.

excellent *Circa* 1970s–to date **UK (NW)**

mitch, v.

be absent from school without permission *c.f.* skive

minter, adj.

a contributor writes: 'at school there was a red-haired lad who complained that he was being called ginger-minger. The teacher, seemingly unaware of what a minge might be and slightly hard of hearing, was nevertheless outraged by the

150

upset caused to this boy and held a special assembly in the school hall. He said that it was no longer acceptable to refer to red-haired pupils as 'ginger minters'.

As a result the word Minter immediately became the most popular word in the school, being used with gay abandon at anyone who had even the merest hint of ginger in their hair. To my knowledge this term of abuse travelled to a number of universities when the boys in that year left school *c.f.* ginger-minge *Circa* 1992 UK (SE)

moh, n.
a person who is bald, The word is pronounced like the 'mo' in 'moth'. The action associated with this word is less violent than the slap: the perpetrator covers the victim's 'slap' (forehead) with his hand, palm inwards, and utters the word 'MmmmmmmmmmOH' in a loud voice, while pushing the victim backwards. However, rapid tapping of the fingertips on the 'slap' can also be used to perpetrate this assault.

A sub-variant of this involves the perpetrator holding his hand in a way that suggests knocking at a door, and making a knocking motion, while saying the word. This may be done by wags sitting at the back of a class being taken by a 'chrome-dome' (bald teacher, gender non-specific), or in a hallway behind a teacher that you know that if you say it often enough, they'll start to cry *c.f.* slaphead UK (I. of Man)

mong/mongol/mongoloid, n.
A person (usu. a child) with the appearance of someone suffering from Downs syndrome. Also a general insult to any excessively stupid or unpleasant person.

monged, adj.
stoned, wasted and/or pissed UK (Scot)

mongoose, n.
an expensive and highly desirable model of BMX bicycle
Circa 1983

monkey grip, n.
the accepted grip used in red rover consisting of an inter-locking of fingers, with the fingernails of each hand digging into the fingers of the other

monkey rush, game
alternative form of 'goalie-when'. Any player can be keeper when in the area but must shout to signify he was changing to keeper. This was a cause of much argument. Also allowed players on the same team to keep throwing the ball at each other & catching it, if they could shout fast enough **UK**

mono, n.
cycling trick involving lifting the front wheel of a bicycle off the ground to ride only on the back wheel – to 'chuck a mono', or 'pop a mono'.**AUS**

monorail, v.
meaning to squat down really low, with your nether regions exposed; even better if you are a bit sweaty/bum claggy, and in a rocking back and forth motion, wipe yourself against something. For example, 'I hope he sleeps well later, I've just monorailed him'. Resembles the sliding motion of its name *Circa* 2000 **UK**

mons, n.
usually seen when a fat teacher wore trousers showing off a bulge above her stench trench, often made worse by a tight belt e.g. 'Mrs Russell's mons is enormous!' *c.f.* stench trench *f. mons veneris* **USA**

moomyang, n.
vaginal investigation by digital examination. Referring to a 'girls' downstairs', and a fella fingering her e.g. 'So did ya get any moomyang last nite?' *Circa* 2002 **USA**

moose, n.
very ugly girl *c.f.* beast, swamp donkey **UK**

morris, n.
used to describe someone who was effeminate or suspected of being a homosexual. The word came from acting like a Morris dancer, limp-wristed or generally prancing around *Circa* 1970 **UK (SE)**

mud baby (to go and have a...), n.
defecate – going for a shite *c.f.* dropping the kids off *Circa* 1990s **USA**

mud flaps, n.
labia – 'they hang low'. Used as 'Damn that women has some low mud flaps!' *Circa* 1990s **UK**

muff, n.
female genitals, female pubic hair, esp. when related to performing oral sex on a female e.g. 'chinning the muff' **UK**

muffy, n.
to break wind, fart e.g. 'Who let Muffy off the chain?' exclaimed after an anonymous fart to discover the perpetrator. Sometimes abbreviated to 'Who muffed?' This expression was used frequently in primary school. However, by secondary school, it seemed to have dropped from the vocabulary *c.f.* air biscuit, guff, fart *Circa* 1990–93
AUS

mullet, n.

type of haircut: short on top (possibly spiky) and long at the back. Subsequently has come to be used in the USA (where the hairstyle is so often seen adorning the heads of those who live in trailer parks) to describe white trash. It is usually yelled when someone who looks a bit common passes by... 'Mullllllleeeeeet!' *Circa* 1980s+ **UK, USA**

mumbler, n.

an attractive girl wearing shorts or jeans, etc that are so tight you can supposedly see the 'lips' moving but can't quite make out what they're saying. **UK**

'munch the trunch', ph.

oral sex performed on a man *f.* munch on the truncheon – alluding to the shape of the penis **UK**

munga, n.

to crack a fat – i.e. get an erection; e.g. 'you would crack a munga over a hot chick' *Circa* 1970s **AUS**

mungers, n.

breasts, jugs, bristols, titties. More specifically the larger and more attractive ones *Circa* 2002 **UK (SE)**

mung rag, n.

the rag or sock or whatever used to shoot your load in. (i.e. to collect ejaculate, or wipe the penis 'clean' after masturbating). Often an unclean rarely-washed rag is called a mung rag *Circa* 1990s **USA**

munt, v.

to vomit, throw up. Perform the technicolour yawn; the five-fingered spread. Call for Hughie etc *Circa* 1990s **AUS**

munted, adj.
(1) usually used in past tense to indicate that something has been wrecked or damaged beyond repair, as in 'You munted my pen, egg!'
(2) 'i drank so much last night, in fact I was Munted.' When the state of being munted is reached, then munters (see below) become objects of desire *Circa* 1999
NZ

munter, n.
a very unattractive female (term often accomp. by 'squealing') Occasionally used in relation to a male, but unusual *Circa* 1980s **UK (SE)**

mushroom stamp n.
mark left after pressing the male penis against a woman's face *Circa* 1990s **USA**

'mutt's nuts (the...)', ph.
very good, excellent. Less offensive way of saying 'Dog's bollocks!' *Circa* 1990s **UK**

N

'Naaarse!', exc.
Squealing exclamation uttered when someone unwittingly makes a comment which could be interpreted as being homosexual in nature, or if a pupil (or teacher) of questionable sexuality walked into the room *f.* corrupt, nice **UK (SE)**

nads, n.
testicles – abbr. of Gonads *Circa* 1970s onwards **UK**

nadgers, n.
testicles – remembered fondly as often being used by Kenneth Williams (who found most fame in the Carry On series of films **UL**

nark, v.
state of irritation e.g. someone could be said to be 'dead narked'. Also used as a taunt e.g. the losers in a game of British Bulldog could be taunted with chant of 'Nark On! Nark On!' *Circa* 1980s **UK (NE)**

neckback, n.
playground punishment consisting of a hard slap on the back of the neck **UK (SE)**

needham, n.
description of a 16-year-old boy – with a mullet and penchant for rock music – who spouts nonsense and lives possible the worst, most humdrum existence ever. That sort of person. *f.* from the 1980s video diary TV show called *In Bed with Chris Needham Circa* 1980s **UK**

'needle-dicked bug fucker', ph.
this is a very serious insult, obviously accusing the subject of having a very small penis. A friend of the contributor lost a front tooth after using this expression on a drunk at a night-club. He first heard it in 1978 but it is probably much older than that *Circa* 1970s+ **USA**

neg, n.
a contributor writes that this is 'an acronym for North End Gipsy. Used to describe the children who lived in the council estate on the north end of town. They stank and often wore the same parka coat for their entire school life. There was one notorious family of Negs who's name was unfortunately 'Negus'.

Other children could identify the chair used by Negs (when entering a classroom the Neg had vacated) because it stank of poor people. These chairs were either isolated or sat upon by an unfortunate child who would be sniggered at throughout the lesson and only later told it was because they had the NEG Chair. Many towns have a North End Gip estate because it is predominantly downwind.' *Circa* 1980s
UK

nem tudom, n.
word used to describe a person that is unsure of their sexuality. Used initially by the Aborigines of Australia back in the 19th century *Circa* Current **AUS**

157

nig/get nigged, n.

to become annoyed (also 'having a nig-on'). Also 'niggy, niggy, niggy' often associated with finger poking or rough head rubbing used to provoke or exacerbate another person's nig *f.* niggled UK (NE)

nimps, adj.

defines an easy task or achievement. Used as 'Geez… I aced that exam… it was nimps'! *Circa* 1980s UK (NW)

nipple gripple/nipple cripple, n.

gripping and twisting the victim's (usu. male) nipple violently *c.f.* purple nurple UK

nish, adj.

pleasant, wonderful. Nice. Done well. Used as 'That was a nish day' as in 'That was a wonderful day' or 'That was so nish, mate' meaning 'that was so excellent, my friend' *Circa* 1990s UK (SE)

nitto, adj.

negative. No. Used as 'Ah, nitto, how's he gone and done that?' *Circa* 1990s UK (SE)

nits, n.

head lice. Because of this also used as a form of psychological torture suggesting someone is 'unclean' e.g. where someone yells 'Nits', and indicates a victim (actually with or without head lice, occasionally no obvious victim is chosen.) Everyone else then makes a point of avoiding that person *c.f.* Nitty Nora. UK

nitty nora, n.

colloquial term for the education services nurse who came around once every six months to tussle your hair around looking for nits (head lice) *f.* Nitty Nora the hair explorer, also Nitty Nora Bug Explorer **UK**

nixies, n.
crossing of fingers (but hidden) to be excluded from something. 'I can't be 'it', I've got nixies' *c.f.* fainites barley pax

n.m.c., ac.
acronym for 'no mates club'. A member of the NMC describes one without any friends. A 'president' is someone with absolutely and utterly no mates. Member of NBNMC = 'nasty bastard no mates club' describes someone who espouses to have chosen to have no mates because he's a nasty bastard. Interestingly these people would take pride in announcing they were a member of the NBNMC. **UK (NE)**

'no stranger to the inside of a chip shop (She's...)' ph.
phrase often thrown the way of any slightly overweight female **UK. (Mid)**

nongy, n.
condom, device used to prevent pregnancy by creating a barrier between vagina and semen from fulfilled act of sexual intercourse. **UK (NW)**

noogie, n.
rapid hitting on the skull with a knuckle, also forcefully rubbing the knuckles back and forth on the top of the skull (actions depend on which part of the country you live) *c.f.* hojo mojo **USA**

norks, n.
breasts **USA**

nut, n./v.

(1) head
(2) to strike another's facial area with your forehead
(3) semen e.g. accusing a female of having performed oral sex with a man by saying 'You have a little nut around your mouth.'

nutjob, n.

a person of questionable mental stability *c.f.* mentler
UK (SE)

nutmeg, v.

the act of a passing footballer playing the ball through the open legs of a rival, making him look immensely stupid. George Best was particularly good at this.

Apparently, this is another example of 'rhyming slang' i.e. 'nutmegs' is used for 'legs' since the ball is played between the opposing player's legs. The person who sent that in said his granddad heard this first in a Spurs (Tottenham Hotspurs FC) training session back in the 1960s *c.f.* skill **UK**

O

O'America, exc.
generally means there could be nothing bigger than, more than, etc. 'big time', 'majorly', 'to the maximum capacity'. Used as, 'Did you see Christine today? She looks like a hottie O'America!', or 'I need to go to the bathroom O'America!', 'That weed got me high, O'America!' *Circa* current **USA**

obs, n.
obstruction in pat-ball, where a dim child would stumble into the field of play thus obstructing one from a fair play at the ball. Similar to 'let' in tennis, but without the rackets **UK**

off ground touch, n.
a way of avoiding becoming 'it' by being off ground when being touched or tagged. To avoid the boredom when everyone stood on the school wall (at St. Joseph's RC Primary School, Upminster, for example), the '15 count' rule was introduced where you could stay off ground for a count of 15 before you had to stand down again **UK (SE)**

oggy, n.
something nasty but fictitious that boys caught off girls by kissing or touching them...similar to 'the lurgie' *c.f.* lurgy
UK (NW)

'Oggy, oggy, oggy. Oi, oi, oi!' (chant)

chant shouted by kids in Wales at any given opportunity to express enthusiasm for something – usually at sports matches. In action, one person shouts the 'oggies' while all around are supposed to join in with the 'oi's'. Very embarrassing when they don't. See, for example, Catherine Zeta-Jones's 2003 Oscar Acceptance Speech.

The Australians have purloined this as for use at sports matches and altered it to 'Aussie, aussie, aussie'.
UK (Wal), AUS

'oh-oh-oh-oh-oh-oh...' (chant)

A contributor writes: 'this is more of a chant than a word. When there was a playground fight, the audience would gather round in a circle chanting "oh-oh-oh-oh-oh..." until there was a breakthrough in the fight or it was broken up. I have no idea why we did it. I know others have told me that "fight-fight-fight" is more traditional. It may be a Scottish thing.' **UK (Scot)**

'ollie, ollie, ollie', song

as in the near-legendary playground song heard in Bedfordshire during the late 70s to mid 80s.

> 'Singin Ollie, Ollie, Ollie with her boobs on the trolley,
> and the balls in the biscuit tin.
> Your'e sitting on the grass with your fingers up your arse,
> singin' Ollie, Ollie, Ollie, Ollie, Ollie
> sing it again, sing it again,
> singing Ollie, Ollie, Ollie Ollie, Ollie
> sing it again!,

There was never a specific occasion for using this ditty but it seemed to have been sung a lot just before final bell, so therefore could have been used as an expression of joy *Circa* 1970s–80s **UK (Mid)**

'one in the departure lounge', ph.
faecal urgency requiring immediate access to a place where you can dump your load *c.f.* turtle's head **UK**

om/om-ertz, n.
contraction of a contraction of 'homosexual'. Contributor explains it as follows: 'By the time I was at school (I started Primary School in '86) "hom" was out of use and had been bastardised to "om" (I'm fairly sure that "hom" must be its origin, but it's a cross with "orrr") and was used when another person had done something really bad/said a rude word or whatever and was an expression of shock – "oooooooomm-mmmm, I'm telling!" The "I'm telling" was rarely absent from the phrase.

Then a new generation of the word was born in roughly 1990/1. My stepsister and brother were playing with the kids of a family friend, one of whom was called Thomas. Thomas did something wrong and my stepsister came out with "Ohmas Thomas, I'm telling". They started using "omas" at school and now it's common in schools across Bolton, usually pronounced "om-erz".' *c.f.* hom *Circa* 1990s
UK (Mid)

oobtay, n.
cigarette *f.* probably from 'tube' (reversed in pig Latin), which was an old term for a cigarette common in southern England.**UK (Scot)**

OOC, ac.
acronym for 'out of control'. Used as 'How OOC was Sarah last night?' *Circa* 1990s **USA**

owie, n.

describes the myriad aches and pains suffered by the young, caused by falls or just the general wear and tear of a youngster's life e.g. falling in gymnastics etc. Also the verb 'owing' used to describe saying 'ow!' (or outch) repeatedly Contributor's mother still accompanies his sister to gymnastics class 'to kiss her owies' as she puts it... real cool *Circa* 2002 **USA**

oxy/oxfam, adj.

cheap and tatty-looking *f.* corrupt. OXFAM, Oxford charity shop and the second-hand clothes therein.

P

paddy, n.
(1) benny/eppy and hence the state of being one adopts on becoming irate
(2) any Irish person

pads, n.
female sanitary-wear. Used to insult males: 'Get your pads off', 'You pad wearer' *c.f.* hammock, jamrag

pag, v.
a lift on the back of a bike – 'Gis a pag!' was a familiar phrase in Grimsby *Circa* 1970s **UK (NE)**

pagga, n.
schoolyard fight or brawl involving lots of people

palsy, n.
person who acted stupidly or as if retarded, or who was clumsy

pankis, v.
hitting a girl on the head with the penis whilst she is performing oral sex *Circa* 1990s **USA**

pantload, adj.
used to describe someone who has a lot of stuff, i.e. when kids would overstuff the pockets. Other obvious reference would be kid wearing a diaper (full) or underpants. Probable origin is from cargo pants kids wore, but now worn by adults as well. Used as 'Man, you got a pantload of candy on Halloween!' *Circa* 1960s onwards **USA**

pant moustache, n.
stray hairs peeping out from behind a female's underwear or swimming costume *c.f.* spider's legs *Circa* 1990s **UK**

pantsed, v.
used in the US. To get pantsed means to have your pants pulled down by someone, i.e. 'Hey look, she just got pantsed!' The (now almost obselete) English word for this is 'de-bagged' *Circa* 1990s **USA**

pantypop, n.
break wind; fart; cut the cheese; bottom burp etc *Circa* 1990s **USA**

paper munchies, n.
describes wads of paper that have been chewed for a long period of time then spat out (usually into people's hair or onto the classroom ceiling). Often an empty Bic biro was used to aid the propulsion of the munchie *c.f.* wasp shit *Circa* 1980s **UK**

'Patsy Palmer and her five daughters', n.
male masturbation (i.e. use of the palm and five fingers). The term is very old (it used to be 'Mrs Palmer and her five daughters'), but came back into general use fairly recently, inspired by the actress Patsy Palmer who played Bianca in the BBC TV soap *EastEnders* **UK (SE)**

pat tash, v.

describes an individual putting a finger down the back of his/her pants, digitally entering their own orifice, then wiping said finger on the top lip of an unsuspecting boy or girl (wimps usually the best option). This causes a constant smell of shit on the top lip of the victim throughout the day. Shouting out very loudly to the entire playground 'Pat Tash' and pointing can achieve added ridicule *Circa* 1990s USA (SE)

pax/paxies, n.

used in playground games. Players cross fingers and yell 'pax' to make them safe from being tagged *c.f.* faynights, fainites barley UK (NE)

peachy/peachy beef/peach, adj.

means good, excellent, ace. Used as 'My new bike is peachy/peachy beef', or 'I let off a peach of a fart.' *Circa* 1980s UK

peanipus, n.

insult. Supposedly refers to 'manliness' of woman, i.e. she is a quasi-hermaphrodite with a penis sticking out of her vagina. Probably began from some callow youth's lack of anatomical knowledge when sighting a sexually excited clitoris *Circa* 1990s USA

peanut, n./v.

(1) a person with an oval, peanut shaped head.
(2) a person who has recently received a haircut
(3) grasping someone's tie with two hands and pushing the knot so tight it resembled a peanut and could only be removed by your mother cutting it off with a pair of scissors.
(4) repeatedly hit somebody on the crown of the head with one's knuckles, as if one were knocking vigorously upon a

door. Usage: 'to peanut' or 'to give a peanut'

peanut smuggler, n.
girl not wearing a bra e.g. for swimming lessons (or wearing a sheer bra under a thin blouse) so her nipples can be seen pushing through her clothing. Boys find this insanely sexy. **AUS**

pearler, adj.
brilliant e.g. 'That was a pearler of a goal by Giggs!' **UK (Wal)**

pebble-dash, v.
pebble-dashing occurs when you have diarrhoea that splatters over the sides and rim of the bowl. Akin to a style of decoration to walls of a house popular during the 1980s which involved throwing small pebbles so that they stick to wet cement rendering. Used as 'I wouldn't use the bog for a while, I've just pebble-dashed it!' *Circa* 1980s **UK (Wal)**

pencil sharpener, n.
vagina, female 'naughty bits'. **UK (SE)**

penny, n.
to drop a penny into someone's drink means that they have to down it in one. If you penny someone who has already been pennied then you also have to down your drink. If you miss with the penny you have to down your drink. Leads to bottles of wine being finished before the starter has been served. **UK (SE)**

periods, n.
general expression of disgust uttered when male pupils encountered spilt bottle of Tizer, strawberry milkshake, red biro ink, red paint etc. Often followed, or preceded, by the word 'Eughhhhhh'. **UK (SE)**

pez/pezzy, adj.
roughly analogous to crap, rubbish etc. e.g. 'Your BMX is Pezzy'. The word derives from 'peasant', so someone who owned something 'pezzy' was naturally a pez *Circa* 1980s **UK (Mid)**

phished, adj.
drunk. Less offensive form of 'pissed' *Circa* 1990s **UK**

picasso arse, n.
woman whose knickers are so tight that from behind she looks like she has four buttocks

'pick a window!', ph.
'Pick a window – you're leaving!' Was used mainly as a specific comment of general exasperation caused by one individual's inane conversation to peers, often a precursor to a 'bundle' or 'fight' or other civil unrest, often involving police, ambulance etc. Generally an unwise remark to make if one wishes to visit whichever premises again in the future *Circa* 1970s **UK**

pie, v.
to ignore, as in 'I saw Mark last night and he totally pied me!' Contributor suggests in might possibly come from 'pie in the face' *Circa* 1990s **UK (Scot)**

piffers, n.
labia. e.g. 'She had piffers down to her knees' *Circa* 1990s **UK**

piffins bridge, n.
the Piffins Bridge is the area of no man's land betwixt the very back of a man's scrotum and his anus. Which is of generally no use at all, apparently *c.f.* taint *Circa* 1990s **UK**

pig latin, n.

a method of encrypting speech, also known as back slang, which involves taking the first letter of a word to the end, then adding the syllable 'ay', thus the word 'radiator' would become 'adiatorray'. Similarly 'tube' becomes 'ubetay', or, phonetically spelled 'oobtay' *c.f.* oobtay *Circa* current **UK, USA**

pig-pile, n.

describes the act of piling bodies on top of each other. Synonymous with dog-pile *Circa* 2000+ **USA**

pig scabs, n.

another name for those insanely delicious packets of highly salted, cholesterol loaded, heart attack promoting snacks otherwise known as Pork Scratchings. These are commercially produced pieces of pig skin roasted in the same way as normal 'crackling' and are utterly addictive.

One of the best parts was when you found one that had a layer of fat attached, or better yet, a little sliver of meat! Deadly but delicious! *Circa* 1970s onwards **UK (Wal)**

pikey, n.

derogatory term for gypsies. A contributor adds '… particularly the type that live in communes of stinking caravans with pyres of junked Mk 4 Granada's and heaps of domestic rubbish left festering on public open spaces. Note: not the real Romany types, but 'dirty, workshy, thieving bastards.' Otherwise, tramp, dosser, one who wears old clothes or someone will stoop to pick up a 2p coin from a street *Circa* 1960s **UK (SE)**

pillow biter, n.

male homosexual *f.* supposedly the pain (or ecstasy) of anal

intercourse which causes the receiver to bite the pillow
UK (NE)

pinch-punch, n.
'game' in which victim was pinched and punched anywhere within reach as 1) a celebration of their birthday, in which case the torture was repeated once for each year of their age.or 2) a commemoration of the beginning of each month as in 'pinch-punch first of the month' accompanied by pinches and blows.

    After the assault, a traditional retaliation is 'a nip and a kick for being so quick'. *c.f.* bumps, dumps **UK**

pin dick, n.
insulting reference to the size of a penis. Often used towards young boys in high school etc. Used as 'Here comes a group of pinnies', 'Don't be a pin dick!', 'He's such a pin.' Also used to 'pay out' on people e.g. 'He's got a pin dick!' *Circa* 1990s **USA**

pipe blocker, n.
description for exceptionally long turd or large number of turds delivered in one sitting, therefore likely to block up the flush pipe of the toilet *Circa* current **UK**

pips, n.
a shout whereby anyone smelling a fart would spread his fingers, press his thumb to his nose and shout 'Pips!'. The last person in the group to perform the ritual was supposed to 'swallow' the fart *Circa* 1980s **UK (S)**

piss-catchers, n.
'Polyveldt' shoes, probably from Clark's. Had this strange plateau on the upper, rimmed by a horseshoe-shaped ridge – perfect for becoming a miniature lake of piss

piss weasel, n.
person with a slimy, sly, corrupt disposition *Circa* 1990s **UK**

plates of meat, n.
rhyming slang for feet. Originally a Cockney idiom now taken enthusiastically onboard by Australians, who frankly butcher the English language at will – though not as badly as the Americans *Circa* 1930s onwards **AUS**

pleb, n.
idiot, fool, brain-dead moron. Often coined as an insult aimed at a person with negligible intelligence i.e. 'Phipps failed Maths again. What a pleb!' *f.* plebeian *Circa* 1980s–90s **UK (Mid)**

pocket billiards, adj.
used to describe the actions associated with stimulating male genitalia through the trouser pockets **UK**

pocket rocket, n.
an erection *f.*
[Ed: I need to explain where the name originated? Really?] **UK**

pole-ing, v.
schoolyard torture. A boy is grabbed by a group and carried to a pole. Two boys hold a leg each and ram the victim into the pole, crushing his bollocks. Stemmed an urban myth that a boy had died from it *c.f.* posting *Circa* 1970s **UK**

p.o.l.o., ac.
polo is the name of a British sweet – originally mint-flavoured, then multi-flavoured. Sold as 'The Mint with the Hole' – so, for people in other countries, these may well be sold as Lifesavers.

Anyway, they were popular so it was common to share

them. This gave rise to situations where one would go up to a girl and ask her if she wanted a polo and then when she accepted say 'ewww, you dirty slag, you want a Pants Off Leg Over ' *Circa* 1985 **UK (SE)**

polo, n.
a bit like the crap kids being able to take random turns in goal. This was an extension whereby more than one person could be goalie at any time. If you were really desperate you got to play not only Rush Goalie, but Rush and Polo *c.f.* Goalie-when, Goalie-rush *Circa* 1970s **UK**

poop shute/poop shooter, n.
(1) anus.
(2) also used as insult as 'Man, you take it up the poop shute/shooter!' *Circa* current **USA**

poon-tang, n.
vagina, also used as 'dude, you are a poon' (scared) usually said with dislike *c.f.* punani **USA**

poot, v.
to break wind softly and subtly **USA**

popeye, n.
either during dinner or directly outside the school gates, along with white dog turds and shredded pornography (if there was a park or alley near to your school), there was an ice cream van that used to sell a Popeye – essentially a small ice cream cone (or 'cornet') but where a Flake insertion would produce a '99'. Alternatively a thin fruit lolly was stuck in (invariably one half of those 'double lollies' which had 2 sticks, snapped in half lengthways).

But also a name called to anyone during the course of 'play' who had something long (stick/ cricket bat/long boot bag) stuffed down the back of their coat at the neck, thus resembling (vaguely at best), said ice cream *Circa* 1970s **UK (Mid)**

'pork and bean', n.
homosexual. Use of Cockney Rhyming Slang. Pork and Bean=Queen *Circa* 2000 **AUS**

porn, adj.
situation, event, place or object that is dodgy, seedy, sketchy or generally reminiscent of the feeling obtained from low budget porn e.g. 'That restaurant was porn!' *Circa* current **AUS, CAN (E)**

pornflakes, n.
dried-up semen left on the bed sheets after a session of sex or masturbation that flakes when scratched. Pun on 'corn-flakes'. Term mainly used by AJ's (army jerks) who watch lots of pornographic movies *Circa* 1990s **AUS**

postal (go...), adj.
to 'go postal' is to indulge in arbitrary unprovoked and usually unwarranted acts of violence. To be 'postal' is to be insane e.g. 'He's postal'. Derived from the violent acts of US Postal workers who, for no apparent reason, go on killing sprees *Circa* 1990s **USA**

postie/hoisty, v.
a lad's legs would be held (one person on each, another couple holding his arms) and he would be pulled so that each leg was either side of a goal post. Pressure was exerted on the aforementioned nether regions until the person screamed. The 'hoisty' was the same as the postie, but a crossbar is used instead of a goal post *Circa* 1990s **UK (SE)**

posting, v.
each of someone's legs held by a different person, then the victim slammed into the metal post of the boy's cloakroom (reportedly the best contraceptive ever).**UK**

pov/povvo, n.
similar to a 'gippo' or a 'piker', but far, far worse. A pov is easily recognised by a home-done haircut, supermarket trainers, an ear stud at the age of eight and a permanent smell such as that of mushy peas, cheese or even urine *c.f.* pikey, gippo **UK**

pranny, adj.
foolish person, a durbrain: Used for example, as 'fuck off, pranny!' Obviously had very vague sexual undercurrent, as sounded a bit like 'fanny'. A contributor writes: 'For some reason, a kid at my school called Julian Van Santen was the prime recipient of the "pranny" epithet, to the extent that his name was changed to Julian Van Pranny. He never lived it down!' **UK (NE)**

prat, n.
(1) an excessively stupid or unpleasant person.
(2) misinterpreted term of abuse at West Lodge Middle School, Pinner, Middlesex in the late '70s, where rumour circulated that it was the proper scientific term for 'a pregnant fish'. Hence common playground dialogue: 'You prat!'; 'Fuck off, I am not a pregnant fish' **UK (SE)**

pricktease(r), n.
girl who excites a man but will not go 'all the way'.

prolly, probly, adj.
shortening of 'probably' **UK**

pudd, n.
semen. Used as in 'It tastes like pudd', or 'Look, he's got pudd all over his pants'. Can be a verb: 'He pudded all over his bedspread watching porn!' **USA**

pukka/pukka J/pukka J Jenkins, adj.
defined as 'something good' e.g. 'That goal was pukka J', 'Oh yes! Pukka J'. The terms 'pukka J' and 'pukka J jenkins' branched off pukka but meant the same thing. Most people said pukka J *Circa* 1990s **USA**

'pull my finger...', ph.
something usually done by males - when you pull their finger they let loose with a loud fart. Usually 'Pull my finger' resulted in chaotic childhood panic, with the person who was asked to do it running away shrieking **USA**

punani, n.
(1) vagina, (as in 'ride the punani'). Recently popularised by Ali G
(2) regarding something as being of high value, (e.g. 'dat good punani bro'.)
UK

'punk, ted or mod?', ph.
question asked by big kids to smaller kids. The wrong response (any) would elicit a punch, although the younger kid could (bizarrely) be let off by shouting 'Smurf!'
UK (W)

puntie-up, v.
like tossing the caber only using a human **UK (Scot)**

puntang/pune, n.
vagina **USA**

puntang juice/pune juice, n.
liquid from a vagina **USA**

purple-headed yoghurt-slinger, n.
penis **USA**

purple nurple/purple herbie, n.
punishment that consists of pinching and twisting the victim's (usu. male) nipple violently. The obvious intent was to do so much damage that the nipple turned purple with bruising or temporary discoloration. It did not usually go as far as that... usually **UK (Mid)**

Q

quacker, n.
woman's pubic area, specifically that between her legs *f.* probably some poor sod who had heard the word *cloaca c.f.* clacker **AUS**

quaid, n.
'Quaid' was the name given to the leader of a rebel army of mutants in the sci-fi movie *Total Recall*. He was the mutated baby that lived as a slimey giant growth on another man's body – not dissimilar to Siamese conjoined twins.

However, a contributor tells us that in the harsh, cruel reality of Lewes Priory School, 'Quaid' was also the name given to the large, boil-like growth on the side of Ben Patterson's neck.

Such was the cruelty of kids that whole conversations could be had with 'Quaid' without even having to acknowledge the poor boy upon which it grew. A typical example would have been to approach Ben Patterson and say loudly "Hi Quaid. How's going?... Oh sorry Ben, I didn't see you standing there". Another example would be to completely ignore poor Ben Patterson as you passed him in a corridor while saying "Hi Quaid".

His horror eventually came to an end when 'Quaid' was finally surgically removed. Although rumour has it that he actually burst in the shower *Circa* 1990s **UK (SE)**

quarm/quarmburger, n.
homosexual **USA**

queef, n.
'fanny fart', i.e. air expelled from the vagina, normally after sexual interaction of some kind **USA**

queg/quegg, n.
someone who has not yet developed pubic hair when all around him (or her) have *c.f.* ham, mallet

quentin, n.
lesbian. A girl who wears sensible shoes *Circa* 2000 **UK**

quim, n.
female genitalia: immortalised in these deeply moving, poetic lines:

> When I was just a little girl
> I had a little quim
> And if I struggled long and hard
> I could get my finger in.
>
> But now that I am old and grey
> My cunt has lost its charm
> And I can get my finger in
> … And half my fucking arm!

UK

quizzer, n.
corruption of 'queer' as in 'you gurt big quizzer'. Possibly derived from bizarre speech patterns of certain gangsta rappers. As with most of these insults it does not so much denote a genuinely gay person much as a particularly effeminate,

poncified or cowardly individual *Circa* current **UK**

qwas, adj.
small amount of something, used as 'Me beer's almost gone
– just a qwas left' *Circa* current **UK (SE)**

quoz/quozzie, n.
handicapped person *f.* Quasimodo

R

rack, v.

kick to the testicles. Racking is when a boy is kicked in the privates. Girls use it as a threat, but many girls have racked a boy at one time or another. e.g. 'Leave me alone or I'll rack you!'. Not surprisingly, this usually has the effect of making a young male take a few steps back out of close range.

rack, n.

female breasts when looked at as a 'matching pair'. Used as 'Good afternoon Miss. May I compliment you on your possession of an excellent rack!' (NB: this sentence is usually followed closely by a smack around the face)

'rack off!', ph.

used e.g. 'Please go away you are annoying me'**AUS**

radge, v.

to have a fit, get angry or lash out **UK (NE)**

radged, adj.

mental, in a daft state of mind. Used as 'Are you radged?' *Circa* 1980s–90s **UK (N)**

radgie gadgie/radgeheed, n.
someone prone to flying off the handle; unstable or crazed
UK (NE)

rag week, n.
that 'time of the month' when a female is menstruating. If a female got aggressive during this (or indeed any) time it would be said that she must be on 'rag week' *Circa* 1960s onwards *f.* university students traditionally hold a 'Raise and Give' (RAG) week, where stupid stunts are performed for charity **UK**

rammy, n.
means a miniature riot. Usual location for these was in school corridors. Situation arose when crowds of children tried to pass each other when there was too little room to do so easily. Usual time for a rammy to occur was between classes and occasionally when people tried to skip the lunch queue *c.f.* bundle **UK (Scot)**

ramp, n.
scruffy, smelly, obnoxious tramp (hobo, not female with liberated sexual attitudes). Rhymes with tramp, first used in a rather delightful poem about an old tramp called Harry Ramp:

> 'Harry Ramp,
> The paraffin lamp,
> Was a dirty bamp...'

f. bamp, tramp *Circa* 1980s **UK (NE)**

ramp (the...), n.
artefact found in most provincial towns, usually a council-built BMX stunt ramp put up in 1986 exactly when the last

BMX was sold, used briefly by skateboarders in the early 1990s and now a hangout for junior druggies headlined on the cover of the local paper every year as 'DRUG-INFESTED EYESORE MUST GO' *c.f.* BMX

'rape!', exc.

schoolyard 'prank' comprising of removing an item of girls clothing (usu. a cardigan or coat) against her will. Or the act of grasping or holding a girl (usu. by the arm) and attempting to touch other parts of her with a spare hand. She would then scream the above. **UK (SE)**

raps, n.

punishment, also 'game' in which one person's clenched fist is held out and 'rapped' with a deck of cards until blistering/bleeding occurs. **UK (NE)**

red route, adj.

menstruation. Usually used in second person as in 'She can't do anything tonight (i.e. sex) she's red route.' Quite common to be used in consultations with patients in A&E.

> Q: Is it possible you could be pregnant?
> A: No, I'm red route.

Circa 1980s+ **UK**

red wings, n.

award given by the Hell's Angels motorcycle club to members who give oral sex to a women who either 1) has her period on him or 2) gets her 'cherry popped' *Circa* 1950s
UK

183

reggie, n.
to grasp and twist someone's nipple(s) *c.f.* nipple cripple **UK (We)**

'release the hounds', ph.
defecate *c.f.* clip a steamer, drop the kids off **USA**

'release the sluice', ph.
at anytime, when things start to get crazy, the sluice is released. It could be drinking, the formulation of a cool plan, or just general excitement. Shouts of 'RELEASE THE SLUICE' is often accompanied by the thrusting of an open palm, into the ribs of your conspirators, your elbow tight against your hips/ribs *Circa* 2000 **UK (NW)**

rem/remhead, n.
someone quite thick *f.* remedial i.e. someone who require remedial reading classes at school. **UK (We)**

remploy, n.
'remploy' is someone demonstrating less than average intelligence/ability. It refers to the Remploy company which provides employment for less able members of society *Circa* current **UK (NW)**

renob, n.
boner spelled backwards. Said this way it confuses teachers *Circa* current **UK**

'ride the short bus', ph.
retarded, mentally deficient in some way. Describes someone the Brits might call an eppy or leper. Refers to the smaller yellow school buses in America that are typically reserved for retarded or special education children. Ex. 'Man, I bet he rides the short bus' *Circa* 2001 **USA (S)**

rikker/rikker action, n.
the anus e.g. 'I split her rickker with me python'. Used in the North West. Rickker action=anal sex **UK**

rim-job/rimmer, n.
orally stimulating the anus *Circa* 1980s+ **USA**

ring raider, n.
sodomite, homosexual, one who indulges in the activity of anal intercourse. Used in the playground to indicate if you are unsure of a person's sexuality e.g. 'Watch him... he's a bit of a Ring Raider.' **UK**

ring-sting, adj.
result of excreting stools heavily impregnated with chilli or last night's curry – not to be confused with the 'bombay trots' *c.f.* bum-burner **UK (Scot)**

ringpiece, n.
arsehole, idiot **UK**

rocket, n.
(Ed: added verbatim – couldn't improve on this)
'One is often referred to as a "rocket" after making a ridiculous suggestion. "Why don't we do our homework at tea-time on Friday then we can have the weekend to ourselves?" "Bolt ya rocket!" "Ya fuckin' rocket!" Do you see? Also a practice of responding to a ridiculous suggestion with a words-and-pictures composition. "Ask your mum to go for the carry-out" would be greeted with, first, "a-rocket!" then holding the right arm at the elbow to the waist and brushing it past the ear (reminiscent of my own school's 'spazzy' motion) in shooing-away-wasp action coupled with loud raspberry. Rarely seen masterpiece.' **UK (Scot)**

'rocking-horse shit', n.
used to describe something that is a rarity, for example:

> Q: Have you got any of those new yellow giant mar-
> bles?'
> A: No fucking chance, they're like rocking-horse shit
> round here mate!'

Circa 1980s+ **AUS**

rock spider, n.
sexual offender – specifically against children **AUS**

rocky, n.
(1) an erection
(2) one who removes things from wastepaper baskets/ rubbish bins, for personal gain. These would include apple
cores, half-eaten sandwiches, biscuits, pens, rulers – just
about anything that still had some function to the Rocky.
These people would subsequently leave school and become
tip-pickers (although this would be largely for monetary
gain, as the intention was to sell that which they had picked
up from the rubbish heap (tip) *c.f.* bag person, scav
UK (I. of Man)

roddy, n.
describes a person who masturbates frequently and openly,
often in public *Circa* 1990s **UK (NW)**

rodney, n.
doing a 'Rodney' on someone meant rubbing, or quick short
strikes of your middle finger knuckle, into the head of the
victim (often a brother or sister). Often used in conjunction
with hair pulling *c.f.* noogie, rooster-booster *Circa* 1980s
UK

roger (woggaaaahhh), n.

term used to refer to someone who was 'not quite there' or stupid. Came from a very bad '70s made-for-TV movie with Julie Kavner (now Marge Simpson) and 'John-Boy' from *The Waltons*. They played two mentally retarded adults who wanted to have a child. Julie spent a good deal of the film moaning 'woggggggah' thus, the word is pronounced woggggah, not 'Roger' *Circa* 1970s **CAN (Ont)**

rooster-booster, n.

playground torture: either pushing thumb between first and second fingers then 'screwing', or rubbing someone's scalp vigorously with a clenched fist *c.f.* beano, noogie, rodney **UK (SE)**

root, v.

to root = to have sexual intercourse. **USA, AUS**

ruggit, n.

someone a little mentally 'ambivalent' – i.e. simple. Used preceded by a big Durrrrrrr (tongue in lower lip) then shouted in the imbecile's face *Circa* 1980s **UK (SW)**

rugrats, n.

little kids below school age, toddlers *c.f.* anklebiters, yukkers **USA**

rule britannia, poem

lyrics to rude old schoolyard songs involving a play on words.

> Rule Britannia
> Three monkeys on a stick
> One fell off and paralysed his

Dick was a sailor
His Christian-name was Jim
His mother took him to the pool
To see if he could swim

He sank to the bottom
He rose to the top
His mother got excited
And pulled him by the

Cock-tail shandy
7p a glass
If you don't like it
Shove it up your

Ask no questions
Tell no lies
I saw a policeman
Pulling up his

Flies are a nuisance
Bees are worse
I saw a doctor
Getting on a

Nurse my baby
Nurse it well
This is the end of my story
And all I have to tell,

This was another version sent in – you can decide which is better...

My old man's a dust-man
'E wears a dust-man's 'at

'E took me 'round the corner,
To watch a football match

Fatty passed to Skinny
Skinny passed it back
Fatty took a rotten shot
And knocked the Goalie flat.

Where was the Goalie when the ball was in the net?
Half way up the post with his balls around his neck.

On came the stretcher
On came the bed
They wrapped his bum in Pedigree Chum
And this is what he said...

Rule Britannia
Three monkeys up a stick
One fell down and paralysed his

Dick was a watchdog sitting on the grass
Along came a bumble-bee and stung him on the

Ask no questions, tell no lies
I saw a Policeman doing up his

Flies are a nuisance
Wasps are worse
This is the end of my silly little verse!
You all smell! Bad!

c.f. arsehole song *Circa* 1950s+

rumble, n.

fight. Often involving more than two people. Sometimes for

fun, often more serious. *f.* orig. USA, spread worldwide by the musical *West Side Story* **UK**

rump ranger, n.
homosexual, also known as a rectum ranger **USA**

runs (the...), adj.
diarrhoea *c.f.* squits **UK**

rusty crotch, n.
female of the ginger persuasion *Circa* 1960s **UK**

rusty trombone, v.
when a women performs oral sex on a man's anus and reaches between his legs and jerks him off at the same time. If you use your imagination, it actually looks like the woman is playing a trombone *Circa* 1990s **USA**

S

sack whack, v.

stand next to your best mate and, without him noticing, whack his scrotum really hard and yell out 'sack whack' *c.f.* fweep *Circa* 1990s **AUS**

saddle, n.

at the contributor's school, and outside, the 'saddle' was given to the passenger, always in response to the request to 'give us a saddle'. At that school they were not normally allowed to bring their bikes, so this was used exclusively during the miraculous week of the Cycling Proficiency Tests, where they WERE allowed (if taking part) to bring their bikes in. The 10 or so pupils undergoing the test would be harangued by the 490 others to 'give us saddle' on the way home *Circa* 1970s **UK (SE)**

saddler, n.

to ride on the back of someone's bike while s/he pedalled in a standing position *c.f.* backer **UK (SE)**

sad/saddo/sad case, adj./n.

commonly used everywhere to describe people who don't fit in, don't have any style, or don't wear the right clothes to be part of any faction. These people are the nerds and geeks of the school world. Sad people are not necessarily miserable, but are often picked on mercilessly, and so don't have a great time at school **UK (SE)**

saddle bag, n.
(1) girl (usu.) supposedly of 'easy virtue', i.e. available for sexual purposes when required *c.f.* school bike
(2) used by women to describe extra layers of fat on their hips e.g. 'I've got to get rid of these saddle bags' **UK, CAN**

safe pub, n.
one of a small number of local pubs that serve children alcohol without requesting identification. Minor customers are generally kept in a very cold backroom

sag off, n.
bunk off school i.e. be absent without permission. Kids sagging off are often said to be suffering from 'saggeritis disease'

salad dodger, n.
overweight person **AUS**

same-head, n.
insult. Based on the supposed similarity of features between people with Downs Syndrome. Used as an insult to peers with less than favourable looks or of low intelligence. i.e. 'you are a complete same-head' *Circa* 1980s **UK**

sannies, n.
sand shoes worn for PE in primary school. They were made of black material with small upper elasticised bit, and had flat rubber soles but, crucially, no laces! EVERYBODY had them in 1970s central Scotland.! An early form of 'trainer' also known as deck shoes or plimsolls by some *Circa* 1970s **UK (Scot.)**

sanny bag, n.

a sanitary towel bag. Paper bags for used sanitary towels, before they went into the incinerator. Often used as water bombs *Circa* 1970s **UK**

sark, n.

slang, as in 'My buddy always talks in sark when he's drunk' *Circa* 2002 **USA (Tex)**

sarky (...git), n.

abbreviation of sarcastic **UK**

satchel, satch, n.

(1) the male scrotum.
(2) an excessively stupid or unpleasant person.

sausage sandwich, n.

sex between a woman and two men at the same time. **UK**

scab/scabber, n.

someone who would try and borrow money or food or PE kit off other people...it was common to hear 'I'm going on the scab' at dinner time... probably from scavenge or 'on the scav' *f.* scavenger *c.f.* scavvy *Circa* 1990s **UK (ME)**

scaffie, n.

refers to garbage collectors, binmen, street-sweepers and other low status council workers. Used in a derogatory way about other childrens' parents e.g. 'your dad's a scaffie' *f.* scavenger *Circa* 1970s **UK**

scam, v.

to engage in close contact physical activities with a partner, usually sexual in nature, i.e. to 'make out' with someone *Circa* current **USA**

scan'ting, v.

humiliation where the underpants are pulled sharply upwards from behind, causing them to wedge themselves tightly up the victim's arse *c.f.* wedgie **UK (SE)**

scan'ts, n.

underpants *c.f.* scan'ting **UK (SE)**

scav/scavvy, n.

contracted version of scavenger. Calling someone a 'scav' implied they were likely to take things that had been thrown away (e.g. 'scrambled' pennies), but more often used a general put down. 'Scavvy' (adj.) was a general word for below par, rubbish etc *c.f.* rocky, bag-person **UK (SE)**

schlong, n.

penis. From Yiddish *Circa* current **USA**

schwoz (going for a...), n.

going for a piss

scit, v.

to mock. e.g. 'Miss... Johnny's scitting me!!' **UK (NW)**

sconner, n.

a person who had failed to begin the growth of pubic hair. This word was only really used by the nine to twelve age group, as everyone over that age had pretty much got over puberty and had moved on to the sexual frustration and terminal boredom of adolescence. The contributor writes: 'I'd love to know if kids at my old school still say it; I do hope the pubeless baton has been passed down through the years. In extreme cases, boys who were targeted as 'sconners' would pull down their trousers in order to display their repost'.

It would seem that this word is exclusively used within

the Black Country, not even venturing as far as Birmingham or Coventry *c.f.* ham *Circa* 1987-92 **UK (NE)**

scooby-doo, n.
rhyming slang for 'I don't have a clue' **UK (Scot)**

scoofee, n.
bastardisation of 'school field' and the general site of games and warfare, such as the tap on the shoulder on a snowy playtime, swiftly followed by eyes, nose and mouth full of ice, snow and dog crap as the hapless victim turned to see his 'chums' (who were usually crippled with laughter once they (the victim) could see and breathe again); great days, great times to be had on the old scoofee, buried under haystacks, mauled at rugby, finding porn, ahhh good times!
UK

scooter, n.
any one who wore glasses and had freckles, based on the character from *The Muppets.* **UK**

scoper/scopey, adj.
euphemism for a person with cerebral palsy, motor disablement, or spasticity; i.e. a 'spastic'. This word was coined as a result of the charity 'The Spastics Society' changing their name to Scope in 1994, to avoid continued association with the common usage of the word 'spastic' as a general term of abuse. However it didn't take long for 'scoper' or 'scopey' to become a common euphemism in place of 'spastic' *c.f.* spazz, flid etc *Circa* 1994 **UK**

scramble goalie, adj.
in playing football, if it was decided it was 'scramble goalie', anyone in the team could save the ball with their hands if they were in the penalty area. When it was 'rush' goalie, it

was only the named rush goalie from each team who could do it *c.f.* Rush Goalie *Circa* 1980 **UK (SE)**

screwball, n.
cone-shaped plastic container filled with ice cream that had bubblegum at the pointy end. **UK**

screwnut, n.
someone who messed up bad. Used as a joke. Often used to describe the 'cool guys' by other 'cool guys' e.g. 'Lenny! You screwnut! You failed English again!' **UK**

scribs/skribs/skribsies, n.
the crossing of the fingers to provide immunity. 'An infinitely better word than pax or faynights. Its origins are lost in the mists of time but it's known to be one true truce word.' *Circa* 1980s–to date **UK (SE)**

scrot rot, n.
sweaty, itchy clamminess around one's testicles caused by adverse amounts of heat and humidity, aggravated by walking into school, wearing nylon underpants and sitting on hard plastic chairs or science stools. *f.* scrotum **UK (SE)**

scrot box, n.
box filled with pieces of sportswear lost by other unknown pupils, that had to be delved into if a person forgot their sports kit or part of it. **UK (SE)**

scruds, n.
new pupils at school. Used particularly of new first formers (year 7) in secondary school – 'The scruds' **UK**

scrumdiddliumptious, adj.
excessively tasty or delicious **UK**

scrump, v.
to have sex e.g. 'I'm gonna get my scrump tonight!'
USA (SE)

scrut, n./v.
the good food or drink, to ingest good food or drink, or describe good food or drink. Used as 'These hamburgers are scrut!' or 'I scrutted that beer.' USA

scully, n.
oral sex *Circa* current UK

scully monster, n.
someone who prefers to give oral sex than have sex by more traditional methods *Circa* current UK

scungee/scungy/scungies, n.
dirty or badly worn and daggy underwear. Prob. originated as a tradename for a brand of 'sporting briefs'. Also has a 'surfie' context but this is probably because the underdaks are worn beneath board shorts *c.f.* daggy, underdaks *Circa* 1950s+ AUS

scutter, n.
scutter, or 'Scutter From The Gutter' to give it its full title, was a name bestowed upon any person who was a little bit smelly, a little bit dirty, and generally wore clothes too small for them and lived in the council flats with their crack-whore mother and wife-beating dad. If you wore trousers that ended 4 inches above your socks, you were a scutter. If you'd worn the same 80s tracksuit top that was 4 sizes too small for you (ironically, back in fashion now!) for the last 12 years, you were a scutter. If you had a grade 1 all-over haircut to prevent catching fleas off your rabid mongrel, you were a

scutter. And you were from the gutter – probably *Circa* 1990s
UK (Mid)

seater, n.
used as a term for hitching a lift on the back or handlebars of
someone's bike *c.f.* backer **UK (NW)**

secret smile, n.
clitoris, female genital area *Circa* 1990s **UK**

sed, adj./n.
(1) great, magic, wicked good. Used as 'That MP3 was sed!'
(2) sexual relations 'I got some sed last night!' *Circa* 1990s
USA (Minn)

'seen my arse', ph.
expression used to demonstrate emotion when upset or
annoyed at someone or something *Circa* 2000 **UK (NW)**

semi-phlegmy, n.
mouthful of saliva, frothed into spit with some, but not
much, snot in it *c.f.* meaty, snot, gob *Circa* 1970s–80s **UK
(NW)**

sesh, adj.
cool, highly satisfactory **UK**

sfinkta, n.
derog anus. Used as 'Get your finger out of your sfinkta!',
'Fuck off you dirty sfinkta!' *f.* mis-spelling of Sphincter
NZ

shag, n.
friend, mate, close associate. Used as 'Ay up shag. Woss
'appening like?' Note there are no sexual connotations to this,

unlike the other more vulgar meaning *Circa* current
UK (Mid)

'shake spunk from a stick (she could...)', ph.
used to describe a very attractive girl, i.e. could even make a piece of wood ejaculate *Circa* 1990s **UK (SE)**

shakey, n.
person whose intellectual and physical capacities are markedly below what is currently accepted as 'normal'. This name arose from the observation that these 'special' people have a tendency not to dance but to stand around 'shaking' at parties and Butlin's holidays *c.f.* spastic, joey etc. **UK**

shame!/showings!, exc.
shout meaning 'You got shown up'. Use of East Midlands vowel pronunciation means 'shame' is transformed into 'shaaaaaaayme! **UK (Mid)**

shan, adj.
shocking or disagreeable (context: 'That's shan, that is...')
UK (NE)

sharon and tracy, n.
names used together or singly and supposed to belong to girls who are often amoral, usually working class, and always vulgar. Made infamous due to The Fat Slags through the 'adult comic'particularly *Viz* **UK**

'sharpen your pencil', ph.
sexual intercourse *f.* put your pencil in the pencil sharpener (contributor says this term is in common use by children of ages 8–10) *c.f.* pencil sharpener **UK (SE)**

shift, v.
to kiss (note: rural Ireland only – not Dublin. In Dublin the equivalent would be to 'get off with' someone) *Circa* 1990s **EIRE**

shiner, n.
appearance of an eye that has become bruised, normally following a punch. Otherwise known as a 'black eye' *Circa* 1930s+ **UK**

shit kickers, n.
boots. Usually referring to Doc Marten's with steel toe-caps, but equally appropriate to any really tough boot as worn by genuine hard-cases, or wannabe ones. So named because they, propelled by the wearer's foot, proceed to kick the shit out of anyone foolish enough to stand in their way. This nickname has, as far as I know, been going for ages, everywhere *c.f.* beetle crushers **UK**

shit liner/bog liner, n.
describes a kid deliberately standing near the goalkeeper (in football) to try to score an easy goal or tap in and claim all the glory *Circa* 1990s **UK**

shit-tickets, n.
toilet tissue. So-called because of the similarity between a roll of toilet paper and a perforated coil of tickets. **USA**

schnazz, n.
politer way of saying 'shit' in any place where 'shit' might otherwise be used *Circa* 2000 **USA**

short arse, n.
derogatory term for someone with 'duck's disease' i.e. their

bum is too close to the ground. Otherwise defined as a person of diminished stature *c.f.* duck's disease **UK**

shreddies, n.
(1) an extreme wedgie: the act whereby several boys gather around a chosen victim, reach into said victim's waistband and all haul up victim's underpants until they ripped. This was (is) extremely painful.
(2) underpants *Circa* 1950s onwards (Australia only)
(3) hairstyle used by (and insult used for) men whose hair is thinning, in a vain attempt to make it look as if it has some 'body'. In shape and form it has the unfortunate result of looking like they have a Shredded Wheat (a kind of breakfast 'biscuit' that looks, feels and tastes like knitted straw) on their heads thus rendering them a laughing stock to all and sundry – except, of course, to themselves. A famous 'Shreddie' is Andrew Neil, sometime editor of *The Sunday Times* newspaper. **UK (SE)**

shrimper, n.
(1) bugger. 'John is such a shrimper, his little dick is never out of Emily's ass!'
(2) someone who performs digital penetration of a vagina in order to be able to lick and sniff his fingers afterwards *Circa* 1990s **USA, AUS**

shwaddapete, n.
used as a substitute for any word between two people if they want to keep a secret e.g. 'Have you any shwaddapete?' *Circa* 1990s **EIRE**

sick, adj.
cool, sweet, trendy. Another from the school of 'reverse meanings' in the mode of 'bad' = 'good' e.g. 'Those sunglasses are great... really sick!' *Circa* 1990s (very) **UK**

silent but deadly (SBD)/silent violent, n.

the silent farts that are always the most smelly. Used to describe a lush anal aroma when no aural experience was encountered. Normally associated with 'He who smelt it dealt it' and 'He who denied it supplied it'.

Another rhyme used after someone said 'the one who smelt it dealt it' was fo the secret farter to quickly retort 'the one who did the rhyme did the crime', and would bask in the joy of having 'won' the debate over the identity of the emitter, oblivious to the tautologically incriminating nature of the statement *Circa* 1978+ **UK (SW)**

silver dolphin, n.

glass marble with a reflective internal crack. These were more highly prized than normal marbles but could be easily produced by boiling in a kettle *c.f.* alley, bomper alley, bottle washer *Circa* 1970s–80s **UK (S)**

siver/syver, n.

basically a drain in the road. A 'gulley' or drain at kerb edge for rainwater collection. Watching *Dr. Who* was considered amusing when they brought on the 'Siver-men' (Cybermen) episodes but also produced some quite horrific nightmares. This was the place where you dropped your 10p for the ice-cream man or disposed of your dead goldfish *Circa* 1970s **UK (Scot)**

sixes, n.

good smacking. When the shout 'Taxi!' went up after someone had farted, someone else would call 'sixes all round'. The 'sixes' were punches from anyone in the vicinity dished out to the farter *c.f.* taxi *Circa* 1980s **UK (W)**

skag-nasty/scag-nasty, n.

someone doing something disgusting or mean e.g. 'don't be

such a skag-nasty'. **UK**

skeet, adj.
small, ill-fitting. Used as 'Your shirt is skeet son!' *Circa* 2000
USA

skeg/skeggy, n.
someone who smelt like a tramp and looked filthy.

skeg, v.
to look at. Used as 'Give us a skeg at that magazine?' *Circa*
1980s **UK (NE)**

skeleton goalie, n.
similar to 'Rush Goalie' but extended to include any member
of the team who would be allowed to use their hands in the
area as any normal keeper would, and also play out-field.
This benefit would apply to a particularly poor team who
needed this added ability to even up the competition. The
opposite would be stick goalie who would not be able to
leave the area *c.f.* rush goalie, fly goalie **UK**

sketch, v.
'look out' or 'watch it' (Always used when a teacher
appeared on the horizon) People were often posted to 'keep
sketch' (i.e. keep an eye out for teachers if something of questionable legality was going on)

skid/skidmark, n.
(1) faecal deposit causing stain of excrement in the gusset of
underwear. This is usually the result of improper bowel control, a wedgie or most often a lack of cleanliness following
defecation.
(2) an excessively stupid or unpleasant person. **UK, AUS**

skiddy, n.
Used in similar fashion to 'gross', i.e. to describe something disgusting. **NZ**

skill, n./adj.
apparently, skill is also 'an African bum disease'. The common retort to a primary school child's self-acclamation of being 'skilled' in a particular faculty, would be a chorus of 'Skill's an African bum disease' (used mostly during the height of the famine in Ethiopia around the area of Morecombe, Lancs, UK). The contributor says they are often shocked at the number of people who haven't heard of this definition of 'Skill'. To this day, aged 20, and not in Morecambe, they find themselves uttering it in a childlike manner whenever 'skill' is mentioned.

I'm informed that the use of 'skill' to refer to an African bum disease started well before the big African famines of the early/mid 80s – and was used in schools around Loughborough/Leicestershire, UK) at least as early as 1978.

Leo of Dorset tells us that whilst he certainly can't confirm whether 'skill' is an actual anal infection in Africa, he can indeed confirm that the same definition was also prevalent in his school in Southern Dorset at least between 1984 and 1989. Also 'confirmed' by 'Henry' in respect of his school in SW London during 1980s.

I'm also informed that when playing football, if somebody pulled off a particularly tasty move, people would say 'skill' in low deep voices. If the move involved making somebody look bad (e.g. a nutmeg) then the person on the shamed end of the skill could reply 'African bum disease' to save face.
Circa 1978–88 **UK**

skilly-wompus, n.
characterizes a mentally disabled or mental retarded individ-

ual (e.g. 'Didn't you used to sit at the skilly (skilly-wompus) table back in elementary?'). Also can be used to describe a idiot or jack-ass e.g. 'Darren's being a fucking skilly-wompus today!' *Circa* 1990s **USA**

skinchies, n.
shout (often accompanied by crossed fingers) creating temporary immunity from being made 'it' when playing sticky toffee, stuck in the mud, tag, etc *c.f.* faynights **UK (NE)**

skit, v.
to take the piss out of someone. Used as, 'Stop skitting me!' i.e. 'Stop taking the mickey out of me' *Circa* 1990s **UK (NW)**

skite, n.
skite means boaster. Used as 'You are such a skite – just because your dad owns the entire free world, you think you're hot' *Circa* 1970s **AUS, NZ**

skitter-jap, n.
person with freckled face *Circa* 1950s **UK (NI)**

skive, v.
to skive meant to skip school, and then, usually, to go and loiter in the park/near a bus stop until it was time to go home. 'I skived school today', or 'he never comes to Maths classes, the big skiver' *Circa* 1980s+ **UK**

skivies, n.
underpants *c.f.* daks *Circa* 1980s **UK (NE)**

slack, adj.
(1) used to describe a girl whose morals seem to indicate she is willing to perform sexual favours on demand. Used as 'That Jenny's a bit slack. All I did was nibble her ear and she

went down on me like Vanessa Feltz on a baked ham!' *Circa* 1960s+

(2) meaning 'tight as a duck's arse'. Used as 'Don't be slack, La!' or 'That was dead slack' *Circa* 1970s
UK (Wal), UK (NW)

slack knacker, n.
lazy good-for-nothing layabout *Circa* 1980s **UK (NW)**

slaphead, n.
derogatory term for a bald guy or person with remarkably high forehead. Also used to take the piss out of girls if they wore their hair up too tight with no fringe. This could be added to by physically slapping your head with the palm of your hand while chanting 'SLAPHEAD! SLAPHEAD!' *c.f.* Mekon, Tefal, Spam Head

slash, n./v.
to urinate. Usually used by men and boys as 'I'm going for a slash' meaning to urinate or go for a wee. One kid at school often had the nickname of 'Slasher', because he was always weeing *Circa* 1960s–current **UK (NW)**

slaver, n.
(1) saliva

(2) to tell a lie or outrageous exaggeration as in 'You're talking slavver' and 'Wipe that slavver off your chin' (accompanied by chin-wiping motion)

slider, n.
anyone who didn't listen to mod, punk or new wave. They were 'rockers' or 'greasers' but worse, they were rockers that had become so 'greasy' they slid! Contributor thinks they could have lifted the word from the film version of

Quadrophenia c.f. mods, rockers, greasers *Circa* 1980s
CAN

slick, slickin' it up, adj.
being immensely cool, something that is the height of cool and the best. Slickin' it up, said to show approval of oneself or someone who is being cool *Circa* 1990s UK (S)

slip gear, n.
familiar to anyone who owned, or knew someone who owned, a Grifter. The bike had three gears, all accessible via a twisty handlebar (very cool): red (for power sprints whilst racing around the block), yellow (normal) and blue (to get you up that steep hill with minimum effort). If you managed to jam the gear between red and yellow, the chain wouldn't connect properly to the cogs, resulting in 'slip gear'. You could booby-trap a mate's Grifter and laugh your arse off as he frantically attempted to pedal away, only to get nowhere and eventually fall over *c.f.* BMX, Grifter UK

slipper, adj.
dirty, badly dressed person. The word is used as in 'I'm not going in there, it's full of slippers' – 'He's a right slipper, he is'. Thought to be derived from the 'poorer estates' in towns where there are always 3 shops – a chip shop, a video shop and an offie (off license). People from the estate would shop, rent a video but mostly play the bandit in the chip shop wearing their slippers – never shoes, they'd walk to the shops in their slippers. It is also particularly used to describe a slipper who usually looks older/younger than they are e.g. 12-year-olds with stubble, or a 40-year-old who looks about 12. Classic-looking 'slippers' are Jack Wilde (the Artful Dodger in the film *Oliver*) who is 12 yet has a full chin of stubble, and Steve Marriott from the Small Faces (the opposite). UK (Mid)

slippy/slip/sliz/slizzy/slipknot, n./adj.
girl who acts promiscuously, acting promiscuously *Circa* 1994 **USA (W)**

slogs, n.
rather painful treatment involved a whack on the upper arm for any reason imaginable – from playing cards, farting or seeing a gas van *c.f.* beats *Circa* 1984-89 **UK (Mid)**

sluggos, n.
underpants *Circa* 1960s onwards **AUS**

slug graveyard, n.
derogatory term for female genital area *Circa* 1980s **USA**

smack-head, n.
(1) heroin user
(2) insult based on comparing person to someone suffering from mental illness that causes them to self harm
(3) similar to (2) but with the implication the person is in fact below normal intelligence levels by virtue of being 'punch drunk' from too many smacks to the head *Circa* 1970s
UK

smeekit, n.
extremely intoxicated *Circa* 1980s onwards **UK (Scot.)**

smeg, n.
exclamation of surprise or disappointment *f.* abbreviation of 'smegma' (a white secretion of the sebaceous glands of the foreskin). Current usage encouraged by 'Lister' (Craig Charles) from the TV series *Red Dwarf* who used it and the associated expression 'You smeg-head!' It has been used in many a playground since. Often used instead of the word

'fuck' especially when teachers were around *Circa* 1990s
UK

smelly belly, n.
person acting stupidly *c.f.* dumbum *Circa* 1987 **UK (NE)**

'smell yer maw!', ph.
used as an indication of disbelief, or sometimes as an insult.
Is supposed to indicate the person using the expression has
digitally penetrated the vagina of the mother of the person
whose veracity is in question. Basically passes on the implication that there is as much chance of the statement being
true as the user having obtained sexual access to the female
in question; in other words; 'I've had your maw!' (mother).
Currently, this is often shortened in use to 'Yer maw!' *Circa*
1970s onwards **UK (Scot.)**

smelly-welly, n.
describes a person from a 'poor' background or anyone with
old, worn or dishevelled clothing – i.e. 'like a tramp' **UK
(Mid)**

smim, n.
cross between a highly conformist person and a flid.**UK (W)**

snag (to...), v.
to spit, usually the green nasty phlegm type *Circa* current
USA

snake charmer, n.
a person who seems to defecate large amounts such that it
curls up in the bottom of the bowl and sticks out of the toilet
water *Circa* 1980s **USA**

snap, n.
(1) general reference to food e.g. 'I'm gonna go home and get some snap' *Circa* 1960s onwards
(2) used to express that one is particularly impressed with an insult that they have just heard. For example:

> Person 1 to person 2: 'You smell!'
> Bystander: 'Oh, Snap!'

Used almost exactly like 'Dee-bo' *c.f.* dee-bo *Circa* 1990s **UK (NE), USA**

sniff, exc.
said while holding your middle finger up at someone. It was popular at contributor's primary school for a couple of years, after somebody learnt it off their older and more worldly brother. *Circa* 1980s **UK (SE)**

snitch, n.
(1) nose
(2) to inform on someone to the authorities (esp. police)
(3) snitch (golden) the manufactured version of the snidge that wizards in the 'Harry Potter' books use when they play Quidditch. **UK**

snooch, v.
fun game whereby protagonists attach a clothes peg to their unknowing victims, thus rendering them 'snootched'. The more pegs you can get on a person without them noticing, the more hilarity (and paranoia) ensues. The word can be used however you want. 'I have snootched you.' Or ' The snootch is strong with this one.' The word originates from the film *Mallrats*, in which a character refers to some bags of weed as 'Snootchie Bootchies.' **UK (Wal)**

snot, n.
hardened nasal mucus *c.f.* bogey **UK**

snot rag, n.
handkerchief **UK**

soap dodger, n.
immigrant to Australia from the UK, anyone of recent UK descent **AUS**

s.o.l., ac.
acronym meaning 'shit outta luck'. Used when someone has had a misfortunate occurrence. Used as 'He's s.o.l.' *Circa* 2002 **USA**

solid (Do me a...), n.
a favour, an act of help or kindness. Used as 'Do me a solid, mate?' *Circa* 1990s **UK**

souping, v.
to give someone a good souping': in winter, if someone fell, or more usually was pushed over, into (preferably deep) snow. With a cry of 'Soup him' or 'Souping' a gang would surround them and kick snow all over them, especially the face and head, until they were soaked. Not pleasant *c.f.* whitewashing *Circa* 1980s **UK (NE)**

'sow one's wild oats', ph.
to indulge in behaviour whilst young that is frowned upon when adult, such as frequent changes in sexual partners. Hence the expression 'To sow one's wild oats all Saturday night and spend all day Sunday praying for crop failure!' **UK**

spac(k)/spaz/spazmo/spacker/spanner/spadge, n.
derog. term for:
(1) a person suffering from cerebral palsy with spasm of the muscles.
(2) an excessively stupid or unpleasant person (also adj. spasticated, spazzy, spazzed)

spac(k) attack, n.
describes a fit of erratic or foolish behaviour. To behave briefly, albeit very noticeably, in the manner of a spacker *Circa* 1990s **UK**

spacco, adj.
'Gone spacco'- behaving in a hyperactive or strange manner *Circa* 1980s **UK**

spacksavers, n.
the sort of glasses worn by 'spackers', 'divs' and 'flids' who happened to have 'double glazing'. Derived from the high street opticians Specsavers *Circa* 1990s **UK**

spam, n.
(1) playground punishment consisting of a hard slap on the forehead.
(2) somebody who displayed a rather overly prominent forehead would be subjected to a rather vicious slapping accompanied by the slapper's exclaimed war cry of 'SPAM!' *c.f.* Tefal
UK (SE)

spam head, n.
derog. term for a person with a large forehead *c.f.* spam
UK (SE)

spangle, n.
(1) a very stupid person, i.e. 'You're a right spangle!'
(2) a 'square tube' of sweets in various flavours *Circa* 1980s
UK (Scot)

sparky, n.
idiot, fool, mentally incapacitated *Circa* 1990s **UK**

spawney, adj.
lucky, jammy, flukey. Usually associated with 'get' (i.e. git) as
in 'That spawney get is so lucky he'd lose 10p and find a
fiver!' *Circa* 1960s+ **UK (Wal)**

spaz chariot, n.
derogatory term for wheelchair e.g. 'I saw a great window-
licker cruising in his spaz chariot' *c.f.* window licker *Circa*
1980s **UK**

spaz cut, n.
haircut which makes the wearer look like a spaz *c.f.* Barney
cut

special, n.
often a synonym for 'disabled' (mentally or physically) people *f.* possibly from phrases such as 'He's a special person',
'He goes to the special school'.

sped, n.
stupid, educationally or mentally retarded, deficient in some
way *f.* Abbreviation of SPecial EDucation *Circa* 1985 – 87
USA

speed bumps, n.
phrase indicates inadequate breast size or shape in the female
sex. Often used to taunt 'late bloomers', skinny girls, or any

female particularly sensitive to their breast size *c.f.* bee-stings *Circa* 1980s–90s **USA**

sperm wail, n.
outburst of sound from male during orgasm **UK**

spew, v./n.
project vomit, often noisily. Also the results of this *c.f.* chuck, chunder

spice, n.
a term for sweets or candy. e.g. 'Can I have some Spice please, Mam?' *Circa* 1970s-80s

spider goalie, n.
see fly goalie *Circa* 1990s

spider's legs, n.
the stray hairs that 'escape' from the edges of a girl's bikini or underwear **UK**

spidoinks, n.
the back page of your school jotter was designed for spidoinks; tear off a piece, chew it up and fire it at the blackboard with a ruler when the teacher's back was turned *c.f.* stolges, wasp shit *Circa* 1980s **UK (Scot)**

spiffy/spiffing, adj.
describes a thing as wonderful, top hole, cool, nifty. Pretty damn good! *Circa* 1930s+ **UK**

spij, n.
chewing-gum e.g. 'gimme spij' *Circa* late 1980s **UK (S)**

spillage, n.

used in anticipation of a fight. Relates to blood loss when someone is cut by whatever means, as in 'spilled blood'. 'There's going to be a fight...we want spillage!' *Circa* 1980s **UK**

spin!/'spin on it!', exc.
you would give someone the finger and say spin. Therefore suggesting they should then be able to spin on it *Circa* 1980s **UK**

spiney biff, n.
derog. stupid or clumsy person *f.* spina bifida *Circa* 1980s **UK (S)**

spinner, n.
describes an extremely short girl. So short in fact, that if you had sex with her you could spin her around on your dick while standing up without her touching the ground. Used as 'That chick is a real spinner!' *Circa* 2000 **USA**

split, n.
to inform an authority (teacher, parent, police etc) of a rule transgression, used as 'to split on someone e.g. 'don't split on me – don't tell teacher!' *c.f.* grass **UK**

split arse, n.
uncomplimentary term for female *Circa* current **UK (NE)**

split the kipper/splitsey, n.
(1) kicking a person in the testicles while two people held each leg akimbo
(2) a game played by 'big lads.' It involved standing facing each other, about 3–5 feet apart, on a grassy area and taking a knife (usually a pen-knife), which you would then throw at your opponent's feet. He would have to (without walking)

plant his foot where the knife landed and pull it out of the ground without falling over. He would then throw the knife at YOUR feet and you would have to do the same. The first person to flinch or fall over when trying to retrieve the knife was the loser. It was basically like a game of Twister, but with the added thrill of possibly getting wounded *Circa* 1955-80 **UK**

spogs, n.
sweets, lollies, confectionery *c.f.* swats **UK (NW)**

spoggy, n.
chewing-gum *Circa* current **UK (NE)**

spold, n.
corruption of 'spaz' *c.f.* spaz *Circa* 1980s **UK (NW)**

spong, n.
a spong was basically a bit of a spaz. Contributor believes it to be '…named after a mongy pupil who caused us to be two hours late home from a trip to Windsor Safari Park when he couldn't find the coach. He got a severe kicking from every kid on the coach as he walked to his seat in the 2nd from last row, when he finally turned up (crying and in company of a lion keeper). 'What a fucking Spong!" However it could merely be a contraction of 'spaz' and 'mong' *Circa* 1975 **UK (SE)**

spoof tube, n.
empty paper towel roll stuffed with fabric softener sheets Used to exhale smoke into when smoking marijuana because it covers the smell *c.f.* flube tube **USA**

spoon, n.
person so dense they were not allowed to use a sharp object,

they could only have a spoon *c.f.* joey, spaz **UK (SE)**

spooner!, exc.
term used to describe the result when a player in a lunch/
break time football kickabout strikes the ball with the shin or
'flicks' with the shoe, causing the ball to arc gracefully miles
over the goal/fence resulting in all players shouting
'SPOONER!' *Circa* mid 1980s **UK (W)**

spooner roundcap, n.
every school had one – the briefcase-carrying gimpy kid,
usually the mummy's boy type. **UK (SE)**

spoony/spoonies, n.
unfashionable shoes. Spoonies applied only to shoes, not to
any other garment.e.g. "Ee used ter wear spoonies burr'eez
gorra pair of Nikes now' *Circa* 1970-80s **UK (NW)**

sprag, n.
the sprag is the one who alerts a teacher or 'grown up' of a
misdemeanour, i.e. a 'tell-tale' or liar who will run off to say
kids are playing 'nervous' or whatever. **UK (NE)**

sprog, n./v.
(1) a semi-affectionate term for a child
(2) expulsion or production of bronchial congestion e.g. 'I
sprogged on the floor'
UK (NE)

spunk, n./adj.
(1) male ejaculate.
(2) courage
(3) an attractive male (AUS)

(4) worthless individual e.g. 'Now listen here, spunk!' (UK)
UK, AUS

square-go, exc.
widely used playground precursor to a sound 'kicking' –
usually followed by '...pal', '...Jimmy' etc., 'be frightened ...be
very frightened!' As a shout, 'Square Goes!' was basically a
call to battle. After a brief exchange of abuse, when a fight
was obviously called for you would challenge your opponent
with the phrase 'Square Goes!' and usually leave a time.
'Right then ya cunt – square goes – you and me – after
maths!' *Circa* 1970s+ **UK (Scot)**

squeeze-cheese, v.
to fart, flatulate loudly *Circa* 1980 – 85 **UK**

squibs/squibsies/squibsy, n.
indicate immunity from being 'it' or 'tag'. e.g., 'No, no, I'm
squibs!'; 'Can't get me, I've got squibsies!' If you were squibs,
you could show it by crossing the fingers of both hands *c.f.*
tag, tig *Circa* 1984 **UK (SE)**

squirts/squits, n.
diarrhoea *c.f.* runs **UK**

squits, n.
mutation of 'quits' with the added benefit of its connotations
of diarrhoea e.g. 'If you give back the fiver you owe me we'll
call it squits?' *Circa* 1990s **UK**

squitsies, n.
to be made exempt from being 'it' or 'had' in chase games.

S.S.D.M., ph.
acronym for Schizophrenic Spasticated Demented Mongol.
The phrase is apparently used to describe people that do not

know how to behave properly and when they don't get their own way act like a spoilt brat *Circa* 1980s **UK**

stagutz, exc.
expression used when someone does something stupid and frustrating. Akin to 'gee whiz!' Used as 'sta-gutz with 'gutz' elongated **UK**

stains, n.
greeting between friends. Used as 'eh up, stains – you orrite?' *Circa* 2001 **UK (Mid)**

stamps/stampsies, n.
an occasional rule of a game of conkers. If someone's conker came off their string, or they dropped it, the opponent would be allowed to stamp on the conker if the owner didn't pick it up in time. So kids would say 'Are we playing stamps?' – sensible kids said no *c.f.* conkers **UK**

steamer, n.
oral sex on a male; blow-job. e.g. 'She doesn't go all the way, but she'll definitely give you a steamer!' *Circa* 1990s **UK**

STD grab bag, adj.
describes a male who has had many sexual partners, and therefore may easily have contracted a sexually transmitted disease from one of his partners *Circa* 1990s **USA**

stench trench, n.
uncomplimentary description of a woman's genital area *Circa* 1990s **UK (Scot)**

stenner, n.
shortened version of Frankenstein. Used to describe a person with a large forehead. Tefal was also used as the word is

based on the large fore-headed characters featured in the Tefal advert in the UK in the mid 80s *c.f.* Tefal *Circa* mid 1980s **UK (W)**

stig, n.
in several schools, in the late 80s/early 90s, it became common practice for the 4th years to read a book called *Stig of The Dump* in lessons. Stig was a hairy Neanderthal man who lived in a rubbish dump and made his house out of treasure such as coathangers and vacuum cleaners. Thus anybody it was felt lived in a dump or made their house out of cardboard became known as a 'stig'. This included any smelly person dressed in Oxfam-style dress, possibly wearing Tesco trainers, and possibly having fleas too. Probably *c.f.* fleabag *Circa* 1970s+ **UK (SE)**

stig-bin, n.
in PE class when you forgot your kit you would have to borrow some from the 'stig-bin', a lost and found collection of manky shorts, t-shirts and lovely plimsolls. *f. Stig of The Dump Circa* 1980s **UK**

stinger, n.
(1) this was exclaimed when someone was whacked in the nuts with a football, or received any kind of pain in the ballbag area. The word was used in Plymouth when someone was smacked in the nuts with a wet tennis ball when playing bulldog.
(2) an exclamation used to acknowledge the pain or anguish of a second party, though often that pain may well have been brought about by the first party themselves. For example, when changing after PE, when some amount of bare skin was inevitable, a person might issue a resounding and painful slap to the bare back of a contemporary, leaving a large red hand mark and bringing about a squeal of pain. 'Stinger!' the

slapper might then say, as if to sympathise with their agony. (3) it was also used to acknowledge pain that was merely witnessed, not caused. Say, for example, if you saw someone go over their handle bars at 30mph or take a cricket ball full pelt to the bridge of the nose, 'Stinger!' you'd announce, with a heavy emphasis on the first syllable.
(4) 'Stinger' was also used in constructions such as: 'Stinger for you!' and the stranger 'Stinger for YOUR head!'
Circa 1980s+ **UK**

stinky pinky/stinky finger, n.
the aroma lingering on the skin after 'fingering' a girl *Circa* 1970s+ *c.f.* fish fingers**UK, USA**

stolges, n.
chewed-up bits of paper flung against a wall (or each other) using a ruler to give extra propulsion *c.f.* wasp shit **UK**

stonker/stonk-on, n.
erection

stott-on, n.
an erection **UK (NE)**

stowed, v.
when the finger was hit on the end with a ball, the finger jammed was said to be stowed *Circa* 1980s **UK**

street, adj.
for kids who aren't from the 'streets' (like homies who get to say Eastside/ Westside), but try to be anyway. No rules as to what is street, but when the group do something different which gets the approval of everyone else, this is labelled 'street', and is therefore acceptable. Typical street things: one

leg up and the other one down on jeans, bandanas Rambo-style, listening and dancing to Old Skool Hip Hop. Street! *Circa* 2002 **UK (SE)**

stress, n.
a mocking exclamation for any expression of ire. Often dragged out, thus: 'Stttt-rrreeeeyyyysssss' *Circa* 1990s **UK**

striker, n.
model of bicycle manufactured by Raleigh during the 1970s, The Striker was part of the Grifter line, (largest to smallest this was Grifter, Striker, Boxer) but unique in that it had a coaster (pedal-back) brake *Circa* 1990s **UK**

strobing, v.
masturbation *f.* the speed of the hand movement. **UK**

stroke, v.
to steal

stroker, n.
person who masturbates excessively *c.f.* wanker *Circa* 1990s **UK**

strotter, n.
young child with no pubic hair, as in 'Har har, Smiffy's still a strotter', usually followed by vehement, red-faced denial on the part of the strotter *c.f.* sconner, ham *Circa* 1979–84 **UK (NE)**

stubble, n.
similar to chinny-reck-on etc, but accompanied by rubbing of chin and a noise of disagreement along the lines of 'neigh',

but sounding more like 'naiii' *c.f.* Jimmy Hill, chinny-reck-on etc. **UK (NE)**

studly, adj.
studly means buff, tough, cool, good looking, popular, just really good e.g. 'This book is studly' **USA**

stuffer, n.
used to imply a person who is extremely self-satisfied, egotistical, arrogant and pompous who will certainly boast about their sexual conquests, but most likely would like to partake in a relationship solely with themselves.

stun/stunner, exc.
basically a word used to laugh at other people's misfortune e.g. 'My dog's just died' – hahah Stun! 'I just got a case of crabs off Shirley Jones' – STUNNER! *Circa* 1985-95 **UK (SW)**

stunt nuts, n.
elongated nuts that went on the back wheel of your BMX allowing you to stand on them to concoct BMX trickery of some sort

suck, n.
to hurt oneself and whinge about the pain experienced. Used as 'So you fell over? Don't be such a suck!' *Circa* 1990s **CAN**

suffering barnet, n.
an unfortunate haircut. The style was usually a result of having been taken to the barbers by one's mother (or perhaps she may have even done it herself) *Circa* 1980 **UK (NW)**

sure bill!, exc.
expression of disbelief, often combined with the action of

stroking the chin *c.f.* Jimmy Hill, chinney reck-on **UK (W)**

sussed, v.
figure out, understand, an assertion of correctness, to find error in another person i.e. 'I'm right, you're wrong'

swabby, n.
someone who enjoys wiping his/her whole face over the woman's clitoris whilst muff diving (oral sex) *Circa* 1990s **USA**

swamp donkey, n.
unattractive person of the opposite sex **UK (SE)**

swamp ass, n.
the effect of sitting and sweating a lot i.e. trousers/shorts etc. get wet and smell **USA**

swankalishious, adj.
the epitome of good-looking and sexy; beautiful. Used as 'She is one swankalishious babe!' *Circa* 1980s+ **USA**

swaps, v.
when collecting football cards or stickers (and similar) to go in albums, you always had some duplicate cards, or didn't get others. You used these to 'swap' i.e. exchange for other cards etc. which you didn't have yet. Spawned, amongst other things, the children's TV show *Multi-Coloured Swap Shop* **UK**

swass, n.
when working or sitting and your butt gets sweaty, you have swass (sw-ass) (sweaty ass). Mostly a male Canadian term *c.f.* swamp ass *Circa* 2000 **CAN**

swats, n.

Pronounced like 'HATS'. A term for sweets and candy e.g. 'Gis' some SWATS!' when the contributor was at school – but seems to have fallen out of favour *Circa* 1980 **UK (NE)**

sweater meat, n.

breast *Circa* 1990s **UK**

sweat(y), adj.

something or someone you found particularly ugly/ unsavoury/ horrible e.g. 'He is SO sweaty!' Sounds best when pronounced in broad Yorkshire accent (with silent 't') *Circa* early 1990s **UK**

sweaty, n.

alternative name for a Scots person from rhyming slang 'sweaty sock=Jock' *Circa* 1980s+ **UK (SE)**

sweaty betty, n.

From the song:

> Sweaty Betty,
> She's like a lump of lard
> Sweaty Betty,
> She makes yer willy hard'

as sung in Leeds playgrounds. Also used outside the song, as in: 'she were a proper Sweaty Betty' **UK (N)**

sweenies, n.

very prominent sideburns. Derives from the British cop show *The Sweeny* in which the main stars sported fantastically groomed sideburns *Circa* 1980–85 **UK**

sweet f.a./s.f.a., ph.

semi-acronym meaning 'sweet fuck all' – felt to be less offen-

sive when used as s.f.a. than in full version *Circa* 1960s+
UK

swick, v.
getting into a queue at the front instead of at the back, primarily because you were older than the rest of the people in the queue and/or you knew the prefect at the front. Was called 'swicking the queue' prompting cries of 'Hey min, get back ye swick!', ' from brave people, or chanting 'swicker' if you weren't going to get away with it *Circa* current
UK (Scot)

swifty, v.
to pull someone's hair back from the forehead (using your hands pressed against their head) backwards across the top of the head, causing pain to the hairline region in particular. Particularly effective if done from behind, on Tefals, or on girls with big spams (foreheads) *c.f.* Tefal *Circa* 1990s
UK (SE)

sword fighter, n.
(1) homosexual
(2) situation where two males both attempt to be pleasured orally (to have a sword fight) by a woman. **UK**

T

taco/taco bell, n.
penis **USA**

taco (going for a...), v.
slipping the face between a woman's thighs ready to begin oral sex on her. **USA**

tagnuts, n.
piece of excrement that sticks stubbornly to the buttock and/or buttock hairs. i.e. those caked on bits of poo hanging from anal hair *c.f.* dookie *Circa* 1990s **UK**

taint/tainter, n.
the small flap of skin on males tucked behind the scrotum and in front of the anus. Origin from 'it ain't' e.g. "Taint quite yer balls and 'taint quite yer asshole' *Circa* 1990s **UK**

'talk to the hand', ph.
accompanied by raising the hand in the general direction of the speaker during an argument or discussion whilst turning the head away. Basically telling someone he can argue a point all he wants but it'll do him no good e.g. 'Talk to the hand, 'cos the face ain't listening' *Circa* 2000+ **USA, AUS**

'talking to god on the big white telephone', ph.

being physically sick, vomiting into a toilet. From the position of leaning over a toilet bowl (big white telephone) and screaming 'Oh GOD', *f.* Popularised by Barry Humphries in his 'Baz McKenzie' comic strip in *Private Eye*. Also called driving the porcelain bus *c.f.* Hughie, technicolour yawn *Circa* 1960s+ **AUS, UK**

tally whacker, n.

penis *Circa* 1970s **UK (SE)**

tampax, n.

(1) a feminine hygiene product
(2) an excessively stupid or unpleasant person.

tammy fight, n.

a yearly ritual on the way home from school after the Tampax lady has been round to do her feminine hygiene talk and handed out free samples **UK (SE)**

tangoed, v.

inspired by an advertising campaign for Tango, a soft fizzy drink, where an orange man would come up behind victims and slap them round the head.

In this case, the perpetrator would run up to their victim and shout 'TANGO!' and simultaneously, with their arms outstretched, slap both sides of the victim's head as hard as possible. It is in this way that one would become 'tangoed'.

This ad campaign caused outrage in the UK and the company were accused of encouraging people to damage other's hearing. The ad was changed, but it was too late. By then it was well and truly part of folk culture *Circa* 1990s **UK**

tankie, adj.

used to describe obese people, i.e. 'built like a tank'. **UK**

tap (...up), v.
to importune in some way. e.g. To 'tap someone up' would be to ask a favour. You could for example, tap a man for a job, or a girl for a date etc. **UK (Wal)**

tat/tats, n.
breasts e.g. 'I'm gonna grab 'er tats at breaktime!' **UK (NE)**

tattle-tale/tattler, n.
child in the habit of 'telling' frequently and generally only for the purpose of making him/herself look superior e.g. 'Billy is a tattle-tale', repeated in a sing-song voice *ad infinitum c.f.* fink, dob **USA**

taws, n.
alternative word for marbles. Often used with 'alley'; 'alley taws' were the bigger marbles that you tried to hit with smaller ones *c.f.* marbles *Circa* 1900-1950s **UK (Scot)**

'taxi!', exc.
The shout before sixes were administered. See sixes *Circa* 1980s **UK (W)**

TB, n.
abbr. Tidy Boiler – an attractive young lady

teacher's pet, n.
someone who seemed to be given unreasonably favourable treatment by a teacher *c.f.* swat, swot **UK**

tea bag (...bagger), n./v.
scrotum. Or someone who sucks another's scrotum.
USA

teapot, n.

effeminate homosexual *f.* the song 'I'm a little teapot short and stout...'. Perform the dance that goes with it, and, when you get to the part about 'here's my handle, here's my spout', think about it or look at yourself in a mirror. **UK**

technicolour yawn, n.

to vomit, be sick, spill-yer-guts *c.f.* hughie *Circa* 1960s+ **UK, USA**

tecks, n.

testicles (prob. an abbreviation). used as 'Shit, watch me tecks!' Contributor said this and 'goozies' were quite popular where he used to live – maybe this is just Cannock Slang and no one else outside South Staffordshire knows it. Fairly well used though *Circa* early 1990s **UK (Mid)**

tefal, n.

person with remarkably high forehead, bald person (from adverts on TV whose actors were shown to have 'high' fore-heads *c.f.* mekon, spam head, slap head *Circa* 1980s **UK (NE)**

telling, v.

consists of alerting the authorities (grown-ups) to some crime committed by a fellow child. Most common phrase: 'I'm telling!' often said in a really whiney way with the first sylla-ble of 'telling' drawn out *c.f.* dob, tattle-tale **UK (Wal)**

ten-pence mix, n.

a pre-prepared mix of sweets worth 1 or 2 pence each that added up to 10 pence. Normally supplied in a small paper bag *c.f.* lucky bag **UK**

ten-pinter, n.

the kind of girl (or guy) that you'd need to drink ten pints before even contemplating having sex with **UK**

tesco's, adj.

playground taunt in the form of a song sung to the tune of the 'conga' i.e.

> 'Let's all go to Tesco's,
> where [Johnny, Marky, whatever] gets his best clothes,
> a la la la, a la la la!'

Taunt implies the tauntees parents couldn't afford 'swish' stuff. Note: for those outside the UK that don't know, Tesco's is a huge supermarket chain which was at one time 'famous' for selling cheap imported clothing of dubious quality. **UK**

tezzers, n.

testicles *Circa* 1980–1990s **UK (NW)**

'the land is yours oh god', song

people used to sing the opening line of this school hymn:

> The land is yours oh God,
> You nourish it with rain.

This was popular because if sang in a certain manner, an all too obvious expletive could be constructed:

> The land is yours oh God,
> You nouriSH IT with rain.

The word SHIT was over emphasised and everyone at Ley Hill Middle School (Sutton Coldfield) was in on the joke... thus making for particularly amusing assemblies *c.f.* Gladly My Cross-Eyed Bear **UK (Mid)**

231

'there's more meat on a butchers pencil than you boy', ph.
used to tell someone they are a little skinny or thin *Circa* 1970s onwards **AUS**

thighbrows, n.
term for the straggly hairs peeping out from a girl or woman's pants if the bikini line isn't shaved to obviate this *c.f.* spider's legs *Circa* 1990s **UK**

T.H.O., ac.
Acronym for 'tittie hard on'. When seeing a girl with hard nipples one would say to his friend T.H.O and the friend would look at the girl passing by and see the protruding nipples. Generally, a secret way for boys to get the word out to each other about visible nipples *c.f.* beaming, peanut smuggler *Circa* 1990s **UK**

thunderthighs, n.
description of a female with large, fat or 'thick' legs *c.f.* keglegs **UK**

tick-off-ground, n.
avoidance of becoming 'it' in game of tag or tick by being off-ground *c.f.* off ground touch

'tight as a duck's arse', (... ducks chuff), ph.
a duck's arse being watertight, the implication is that the person described is extremely mean or stingy with money – insult often applied to persons of Scottish descent *Circa* 1960s+ **UK (Wal)**

timmy, n.
insult with inference that the target is in some way mentally

or physically handicapped *f.* 'Timmy' – wheelchair-bound character in *South Park* cartoons *Circa* 1999 **UK**

tingle-tangle, n.
often, during a game of conkers, a particularly vicious attempt at a hit would result in the shoelaces/strings becoming entwined. At this point the two kids playing would tug furiously at each other's conker, and should one conker be pulled from the other and onto the floor, the mass of kids watching would jostle for position to stamp on the conker rendering the game over. Usually upset horribly the conker's owner as it had probably been varnished and baked and all sorts *Circa* 1970s **UK (Mid)**

tin-grin, n.
rude name for someone wearing braces on their teeth *c.f.* brace-face, metal-mouth **USA**

tipsies, n.
part of game of 'slaps'. Called by the slapper in a game of slaps to refer to the fact that although the slappee moved his hands out of the way, the slapper's finger-tips caught the victim's hands, thereby entitling the slapper to another shot *(Ed: Question – who played the 'free slap' rule, where if the slappee flinched 3 times when the slapper was bluffing, you got a free slap?)*
c.f. slaps, knuckles **UK (I. of Man)**

titanic, n.
a lady who goes down first time out. **UK**

tit (blue...), n.
alternate name for a British Policeman's helmet *f.* pointy shape with nipple-like protruberance on top (Also used on TV show *The Young Ones* c. 1983 when Neil joins the Force.

'Come in Neil, take the tit off your head') *Circa* 1980s to date **UK (Mid)**

tit spanners, n.
hands i.e. 'Keep your tit spanners off my lunch!' *Circa* 1970s **S. Africa**

titted, v.
the result of feeling up a girl in the playground *Circa* 1980s **UK**

titty twister, n.
to grab a nipple and twist violently *c.f.* purple nurple etc. **USA**

'toast!', exc.
form of taunting used when classmate loses a game or answers something wrong. Said in a drawn out way, therefore making it more annoying. Often accompanied by saying 'burn', in the same manner, for effect *Circa* 1980s **USA (Cal)**

todger/tadger, n.
euphemism for penis *Circa* 1950s onwards **UK**

todger dodger, n.
lesbian. One who does not like willies so therefore dodges them.

toe jam, n.
yukky smelly stuff that results from athletes foot

toe-rag, n.
literally a piece of cloth used to clean between the toes and therefore quite probably scruffy and smelly. Phrase used by teachers and boys at secondary school in Lincolnshire, espe-

cially the headmaster Mr. Sykes, who would often say 'You're a toe-rag lad – no I'll change that, you're an intelligent toe-rag' **UK (NE)**

toffo, n.
another term for sexual intercourse. Convoluted, if obvious, derivation using rhyming slang from a 1960s and earlier, UK Toffee confection called 'Toff-o-Lux'. Rather like Rolo's, i.e. in 'tube' form, but made of hard toffee and no chocolate coating *Circa* 1960s onwards **UK (SE)**

togger, n.
soccer (association football) *Circa* 1960s **UK (Mid)**

toley, n.
essentially a toley is a jobby and the application of the word means that insults follow like jobby/shit/shite. A classic dignity stripper.

However, toley is rather more personalised and is perversely more effective for being less abrasive. Whereas 'shit' may in some cases be construed as good (the classic 'this is good shit man') there is no positive derivation of toley – it is wholly negative in its connotation. Toley is a word that is often used to greatest effect as part of a more creative insulting ramble e.g 'Fuckin' useless toley prick' **UK**

tommy tank, n.
rhyming slang for masturbation, i.e. Tommy Tank = wank. Derived from the children's TV programme *Thomas the Tank Engine Circa* 1980s **UK (Mid)**

tonsil hockey, n.
a passionate form of 'french kissing', i.e. a form of mouth-to-mouth contact which includes the intertwining of tongues so forcefully that one can be said to be pushing it literally

against the partners tonsils *c.f.* french kissing *Circa* 1960s
UK

tool, n.

(1) euphemism for penis.
(2) a fool, an idiot. Derogatory comment used in some parts
of Australia since about 1996. Used internationally for 50
years or more. **AUS**

toot, v.

to watch or guard against discovery by teachers e.g. 'keep
toot while I nick the sandwiches from this lunch box' *Circa*
1990s **UK**

torpedo, n.

a male penis which is wide at the base and gradually
becomes skinnier as you move toward the head **USA**

totty, n.

attractive female *c.f.* tidy boiler **UK**

toss arse, n.

a tosser i.e. a person who masturbates frequently

'totally tasty thermal pastry', ph.

used in the description of something being very 'cool' or
awesome, used most commonly in reference to really good
food or some event that has happened to you that benefits
you in some way. Sometimes used in the shortened form of
'totally tasty' or '3tp'.

Never used with sexual connotations, but sometimes is
mistaken to be when 'totally tasty' is left out. Because then it
becomes 'thermal pastry' which has been known to refer to
the place between a woman's legs, and its uses when not cov-

ered in clothing *Circa* 1990s **UK**

touching cotton/touching cloth, ph.

describing faecal urgency i.e. really having to go to the bathroom to defecate (as in, a turd is just beginning to touch the cotton/cloth of your underwear.) Used as 'Dude, I'm touching cotton... I'll be right back' *c.f.* turtle's head *Circa* 2001 **CAN**

'tough titty', ph.

hard luck **USA**

townie, n.

similar in definition to Chatham Chav, Kappa Slappa, Essex Girl, Shazza etc. Typically girls who wear Reebok trainers, Kappa sportswear, white puffa jackets, clowns (a really foul type of jewellery which involves a gold, jewelled, preferably moveable, clown – yes, a clown – the bigger the better hanging off a gold chain), lots of reeeeeally tacky 'Ratners'-style gold jewellery and hair which can sport any of the following hairstyles – plastered to head with a small thin section curled, styled and forced to hang next to face; the pineapple (hair in pony tail right on top of head); extravagant bun (very long hair twisted into an over-exaggerated bun) – all of these hairstyles MUST use a gold scrunchie and as much gel as is humanly possible.

These girls normally get pregnant by the age of 12 and have boyfriends called Gazza and Kevin. I know you've seen them walking down the street – sadly, everyone has had this particular misfortune at some time in their life.

tpt, n.

abbreviation of 'trailer park trash' – i.e. poor and quite possibly married to a close family relative. **USA**

trabs, n.
trainers *Circa* 1980s **UK (NW)**

trackstand, v.
BMX or Trial Bike stunt. Involves standing on the bike when it is stationary, keeping balance for as long possible without touching the ground or moving. Slight adjustments can be made by pedalling or moving the handle-bars *Circa* 1980s **UK**

treeing, v.
at the contributor's secondary school they had a grass banking used for sunbathing on hot summer days. Sunbathing was, however, fairly risky as it was likely that a group of two or more boys would grab your legs (usually without warning) and drag you down the banking into one of the many trees impacting with legs on either side the tree.

There were only two defences against this:

1) Rolling onto your stomach so your legs were twisted. This protected your testicles but caused nasty injuries to the inner legs due to the speed of impact (normally a full run)

2) Putting your hands in the way before impact. This sometimes failed due to the force of the impact or was not an option if the group of boys grabbed your arms as well as your legs *Circa* 1990s **UK (NE)**

trench-hook, adj.
insulting the appearance of a penis by saying looks like a capital 'L' *Circa* 2000 **USA**

trev, adj.
stereotypical brain-dead teenage yob, usually wearing baggy jeans and a bomber jacket and carrying a record bag, often with a 'Technics' logo *Circa* 1990s **UK (SW)**

tricolore, n.

Not really 'slang' but interesting nevertheless – quoted verbatim:

"Not exactly a word, this was the French textbook loads of people learnt French from. There were a number of things we found amusing such as the guy who always asked *'Est-ce-qu'il-y-a une banque pres d'ici?'* in a voice so deep it made Mr Bean sound like Joe Pasquali. The reason for this, we realised, must be due to the fact that the Tricolore audio cassettes were recorded by two blokes, and since any women's voices were just a bloke talking in a high-pitched voice, they had to make the bloke's characters obvious – consequently they all had deep voices. This was not helped by the fact that our French tapes were all played on the standard 'School-Issue' Coomber cassette player with a big black woven-grille front and a wooden back with holes drilled in it. These cassette players invariably resonated erratically no matter what kind of sound was being played.

Some common Tricolore Phrases:

> *'Comment??'*
> *'Oui, Madame, il-y-a une banque la-bas.'*
> *'Numero UN! Sex-ion A! EX-OM-PLUH!'*

Of course, all our books dated back to the seventies so when I was at school in the mid-nineties you couldn't see the photos due to the 'modifications' that other students had made over the years. I remember the 'Woman-With-The-Petrol-Pump' photo was the most graffitied." **UK**

trouser snake (the one-eyed ...), n.
the penis **AUS**

trump, n./v.
emission of wind or the act of passing wind. Interchangeable

use e.g. 'Errrgghhhh who's trumped?', or 'Who made that trump?' Presumably a contraction of trumpeted, and reference to outdoing the other nasal offerings currently around! *c.f.* fart *Circa* 1990s **USA**

trunter, n.
derogatory term for an unattractive, overdone older female. 'Gawd, look at the state of that old trunter'. Found in abundance at so-called 'grab a granny' nights at dubious venues *Circa* 1980s **UK (SE)**

truprint, n.
to press the sole of your shoe against the black trousers of your mate, thus leaving behind a perfect dusty footprint *c.f.* chalking **UK**

tube, n.
vagina. Used as an insulting term as a substitute for cunt or fanny. Used as 'You're a tube, by the way!' Often used at the start of exchanges that lead to a minor scuffle, later to be talked about as if it had been the Rumble in the Jungle *Circa* 2000 **USA**

turd burgler, n.
male homosexual **UK**

turd tapper, n.
male homosexual **CAN**

turtle's head, n.
desperate faecal urgency, when faeces begins to protrude from the anus. This allegedly looks like a turtle's head emerging from its shell. Used as 'Aw shite man, I have to go NOW – I've got the turtle's head' *c.f.* touching cotton *Circa* 1970s

onwards **UK (Scot)**

'tutankhamun!', exc.

accompanied by stroking of a chin the length of a walking stick to imitate the famous image of the boy-Pharaoh's death-mask, this was a refinement of the chinny reck-on method of indicating disbelief *c.f.* chinny reck-on *Circa* 1980s-90s **UK (E)**

twag, v.

play truant *c.f.* bunk, mitch, skive *Circa* late 1970s **UK (NE)**

twag lady (man), n.

someone who drives around looking for truants *Circa* late 1970s **UK (NE)**

twang-twang, v.

assertion of conceit in another (accompanied by flicking imaginary moustache) *Circa* 1970s **UK (SE)**

twat, n.

(1) vagina
(2) excessively stupid or unpleasant person
(3) at Elizabeth Woodville Primary School in Leicestershire, they thought the proper definition of twat was 'pregnant goldfish'. They cannot be blamed for this, as the poet Robert Browning made a similar error of judgement, guessing that the word meant some part of a nun's attire. A-level English was considerably lightened by the discovery of these classic lines in *Pippa Passes*:

> 'Then, owls and bats, cowls and twats,
> Monks and nuns, in a cloister's moods,
> Adjourn to the oak-stump pantry!'

twat, v.

an alternate meaning to the sexual version. Here the meaning is to hit someone quite hard, or beat them up. Commonly used in the past tense i.e. twatted *Circa* 1970s+ **UK**

twatman, n.

an excessively stupid or unpleasant person *f.* TWAT + BATMAN

two-ball screwball, n.

ice cream with bubblegum in the bottom in a Dalek-shaped plastic cone. Filthy name, and rumoured to contain LSD.

two-dicks, n.

derog. an idiot, a very stupid person, used to describe a person who is such a wanker he must have two dicks as one wouldn't be enough to make him that bad.
c.f. thick as two short planks **AUS**

twocker/twok/twoc, n.

originally described a car thief, often 'ram raider' or 'joyrider' but eventually coming to mean anyone a bit dodgy, as in 'he's a bit of a twocker, but he's alright' *f.* police term Taken Without Owners Consent *Circa* 1989 **UK (NE)**

two Irishmen, rh.

yet another rhyme based on similarities between endings and beginnings of words:

> Two Irishmen, two Irishmen were digging a ditch
> One called the other one a dirty son of a...
> Peter Murphy had a dog, a very fine dog was he,
> He gave it to his lady friend to keep her company,
> She fed it, she taught it, she taught it how to jump,
> It jumped right up her petticoat and bit her on the

Country boy, country boy sitting on a rock
Along came a bumblebee and stung him on his...
Cocktail, ginger ale, five cents a glass...
If you don't like my story you can shove it up your...
Ask me no questions, tell me no lies
If you ever get hit with a bucket of shit,
Be sure to close your eyes

Circa 1980s **UK**

two world wars, song
a contributor writes: "It wasn't unusual for our school to have foreign exchange students on a fairly regular basis. If it was learnt that any of these children were German, they were pointed at and had the following song chanted at them:

Two world wars and one world cup,
doo dah, doo dah.
Two world wars and one world cup,
doo dah, doo dah day.

UK

U

ummaa (and similar), ph.
usually used when witnessing or hearing of another's wrongdoing e.g. Someone drops a glass of milk: 'Ummaa, look what you did'. A kid might punch another: 'Umma, I'm dobbing' was used heaps! Usually put the speaker in a place of authority: they know it was wrong and that knowledge is power.

In infants school in Croydon, 'ummm' was short for 'ummm, I'm telling' (probably only ever uttered by little girls) and featured in the following rhyme:

> Ummm, umm
> I'm telling my mum
> You showed your bum
> In front of me

USA, UK, NZ

unit, n.
to be 'Unit' was to be strange in some way – if anyone did anything odd they had 'Unit' chanted at them for a while. It's roughly equivalent to 'Joey', said in two deliberately long syllables as 'Uuuuu-nittttt' *f.* Special Needs Unit
(Ed: although having looked at this a few times it dawned on me they might have been saying 'You nit' – doh!)

c.f. Joey, Spaz *Circa* 1970–80s **UK (SM)**

USA, n.
'Under Skirt Area', or 'Up Skirt Action' **USA**

u.t.a., ac.
acronym for Up The Arse. A way of telling someone where to stick their request, instruction, order etc. that can be used in polite society *Circa* 2000 **USA**

V

vadge/vaj, n.
(1) the female vagina. Insult in the vein of 'You're a fanny'
e.g. 'Ya fuckin' vaj!' Sometimes elaborated upon to produce
the eclectic 'vaj-badge' for purely poetic reasons only
(2) an excessively stupid or unpleasant person **UK**

vainites, n.
word shouted to give you protection and exclude you from
attack during a game of British Bulldog etc. *c.f.* faynights,
fainites barley **UK**

vagina decliner, n.
male homosexual

vee dub, n.
female genitalia when shaved. So named from the shape of
the Volkswagen Beetle bonnet e.g. 'I screwed Jennie last night
– did you know she was vee dubbed?' **USA**

vegemite valley (travelling up the...), n.
anus/rectum (usu. with homosexual connotations) *f.* possible source of Vegemite? *c.f.* Marmite motorway
AUS

velcro, n.
lesbian. Refers to attraction of pubic hair *Circa* 1990s
USA

verse/versing, v.
to compete against, as in sports e.g. 'We're versing the Mets
in our first game.' Heard around schools in Seattle *f.* abbreviation of versus **UK**

vick/vicky (flick the ...), n.
to stick your two fingers up at someone in a manner meant
to be insulting e.g. 'I gave that maths teacher the vick this
morning' **UK**

vinegar strokes, n.
said to be the last strokes of sexual intercourse or masturbation immediately prior to ejaculation *c.f.* gravy strokes

viper neck grip, n.
tight squeeze on the back of the neck of an unsuspecting victim. Grip is usually made by the thumb separated from the
other four fingers. The fingers are then formed around the
back of the victim's neck and pressure is applied, usually
causing the victim to scrunch shoulders up and cause the
release of the shocking grip. Be careful, friends have become
enemies over this attack! *Circa* 1970s **USA**

vut, n.
idiot or person considered to be unworthy, a loser *Circa*
1990s **UK (S)**

W

wabs, n.
breasts *Circa* 2002 **USA**

wack, n.
the whole way/load. 'He was so scared he cakked his wack'
UK (Mid)

wagner, n.
used to disguise the word wanker. In this way, you could call
someone a wagner in front of a teacher and they couldn't do
you, when really you meant wanker. It is mostly used when
in class near a teacher or figure of authority *Circa* 1980s+
UK (SE)

wallace and gromit, v./n.
vomit. Rhyming slang *c.f.* hughie, barf etc. **UK**

wallob, adj.
used to describe small fat kids with hairy bodies. Often
referred to as beasts or ogres, *Circa* 1980s **UK**

wally, n.
someone daft. **USA**

wankchops, n.
a general insult. Used by the contributor to refer to 'an over-weight balding, camp yet marginally evil neighbour who would take an unnecessarily long time to return our stray balls from his garden – "What a wankchops!"' *Circa* 1980s **UK**

wankshaft, n.
vulg. the male penis

wankpiece/tosspiece, n.
person of a high idiotic status who has committed an act of extreme slackness or stupidity. A higher form of a tosser or wanker *Circa* 2000 **UK**

wankstain, n.
vulg. insult. Comparison between recipient of insult and stains left by semen.
UK (Mid)

wank tanks, n.
testicles **UK**

waps, n.
corruption of the word baps (meaning breasts) Used because 'girls on the street would know if you turned to your mate and said "she's got nice baps". Now you can turn to your mate and say "Rob, has our mobile got wap?", to mean "Have you noticed the nice waps going by?". Alternatively there's the less subtle "Wap attack!" Either way it sounded cool to say even if the girls found out what you were talking about' *Circa* 2002 **UK**

wasp shit, n.
get a bit of paper, shove it in your mouth. Chew until the con-

sistency is correct. Then chuck it against the wall. The walls at the contributor's school in Luton, Bedfordshire, were literally plastered with Wasp Shits. It really kicked off about 1983-84 and was still going strong in '87 when he left.

Closest he ever saw someone come to getting caught for making Wasp Shits was a lad who had shoved a whole sheet of A4 in his mouth mid lesson, just as the teacher asked him a question! Somehow or other he managed to get through the ordeal by making grunting noises.

Some of the kids used the term 'Consistency', but Wasp Shit was the preferred definition *Circa* 1983–87 **UK (SE)**

water-melon, n.
large and long lasting gob-stopper packaged in a box

wazz/whiz, n./v.
either urine itself, or the act of urinating. Basically an alternative to 'piss'. Used as 'I'm going for a wazz'. Seems to be more popular among females than males *Circa* 1980s–90s **USA**

wazzock, n.
idiot, fool, twat. Possibly created by comedian Mike Harding during the 1970s *c.f.* twat **UK**

'wazzup?', ph.
mutation of 'What's up', which itself is a contraction in meaning of 'Hello! What are you doing? Is anything interesting happening?' *Circa* 1990s **UK**

wedding tackle, n.
male genitalia *c.f.* family jewels, meat and two veg **UK**

wedgie, n.
humiliation whereby the underpants are pulled sharply

upwards from behind, causing them to wedge themselves tightly up the victim's arse.

Variations:

Pure wedgie:
The victim is only wearing underpants when the attack occurs, thus inflicting a much greater amount of embarrassment than normal.

Super wedgie:
Pure wedgie, but with the assailant then grabbing the crotch of the victim's underpants (from behind as it is exposed) and continuing to pull, resulting in the victim's genitals being revealed. (This is particularly embarrassing if the victim is not quite flaccid.)

Wedgie war:
All-against-all with lots of ganging up, normally in a swimming pool. A good attack is considered to be when the victim is lifted out of the water by his swimming togs to at least his knees. (Note that this activity can be very deleterious to the well-being of swimming togs.)

Wedgie-proof:
The victim's underpants are so stretchy that the wedgie doesn't hurt, or they are wearing Speedos, which tend to just stretch instead of heading painfully for the butt-crack. Can refer to the person or the apparel.

Atomic Wedgie:
Trying to get the victim's pants over their head.

(Ed: wedgies of the atomic variety tend to be a grey area, and are difficult to define.

The children's' cartoons of recent times tend to define 'atomic wedgie' as a wedgie where the underpants are pulled up to such an extent that the elastic band could then be put around the victim's head. This, of course, is pure bullshit, and cannot occur in the real world (unless, of course, the victim's underpants are made of that magical, non-existent elastic). But this perhaps is the origin of the real-life atomic wedgie.

In an attempt to achieve the around-the-head-with-the-elastic-band state, one will pull the underpants of the victim to the point of ripping either the elastic band or the fabric of the underpants. Some will perhaps argue that cartoons have nothing to do with this term, and that atomic wedgies have no intention of going around the head, but just to rip the underpants. Either way, I'm sure it sucks to get one of these. It's interesting that I take the term 'atomic wedgie' in an entirely serious manner.)

We received the following communication from Andrew Jordan:

'I feel duty-bound to point out that you refer to the forceful pulling of pants up into an arse-crack as a "wedgie" – as a purist, I think you should also include the UK term for the "wedgie", namely the "Johnny Clegg" or to "Clegg" some-one. You must have heard that?'
UK, USA, NZ, AUS, CAN

> **wedgie-gang, n.**
> group-wedgie-ing. Kids who left school at 16 rather than staying on to go to 6th form who would walk

around the playing fields/yard during the last week of school in gangs and give wedgies to any first years' they found *c.f.* scan'ting, shreddies, wedgie **UK (NE)**

wedgie-kegger, n.
term of general abuse. Although a precise definition is elusive, it was clear from the daily usage in my school that the meaning was both specific and insulting. It was essential that the phrase 'you wedgie kegger' was uttered in a shrill, nasal tone, and it was broadly understood to have something to do with smelly pants, perhaps originating from the separate slang phrase 'kegs', meaning pants, and 'wedgies', i.e. the practice of yanking said pants right up the crack of one's unsuspecting victim **UK**

weedon, adj.
to be in a strop or to be annoyed **UK (SE)**

weeor, exc.
if somebody fell over then you would shout 'weeor!' and flick your fingers outward from a fist *Circa* 1990s **UK (NW)**

wep, n.
weak, insipid or uninspiring female *Circa* 1980s-90s
UK (NW, Wal)

weird beard, n.
scruffy beatnik type, or someone who looked like they were a Greenpeace or CND supporter **UK**

wet willie, v.
finger covered in spit is forced into someone's ear and twist-ed. This sounds and feels disgusting to the victim. It was

popularised in the UK following an episode of *The Simpsons* which showed Bart getting one **UK**

'wheesht!', exc.
pronounced as it is spelt. Means to shut up and be quiet *Circa* 2002 **UK**

'whellah!', exc.
exclamation at the conclusion of a list of chores or steps leading up to an end result. Similar to presto, or eureka.
USA

whigger, n.
adolescent male of Anglo-Saxon descent who acts out with African-American stereotypes e.g. listens to rap in his low rider so everyone for blocks can hear it, speaks fluent Ebonics, wears overlarge gold jewellery, wears a cap on most occasions in the inverted position, and almost always has a toothpick dangling between his teeth. Basically a wannabee Afro-American and a suburban US phenomenon *f.* obvious derivation from racial slur *Circa* 1986-90 **USA**

'whistle for your nipple', ph.
'fun game'. Involves firmly gripping the nipple of a compatriot and shouting 'Whistle for your nipple'. The painful grasp is only released when the victim manages to whistle – which is nigh on impossible due to extreme pain and/or mirth (just try it) *c.f.* nipple cripple **UK**

whitewashing, v.
during the winter (when there is snow or ice on the ground), the action of tripping someone over and then getting as many people as possible to gather and kick as much snow/ice/slush over them as possible – or just kick them *Circa* 1983-90 **UK (NE)**

wicked, adj.
really good, fantastic, excellent. Another in the spate of
bad=good slang words *Circa* 1990s **UK**

wide/wide'o, n.
describes people who won't give you what you want i.e.
juice, crisps, sweets, a puff on a cigarette and so on, but also
used to describe anti-social actions, like chucking schoolbags
into fields. Used as:

> 'Gies a drink of your Coke?'
> 'Naw!'
> 'Dinna be wide!'

Circa current **UK (Scot)**

wife beater, n.
sleeveless shirt *Circa* 1990s **USA**

willy operation, n.
a group of pre-pubescent boys, while in a state of undress
before/after a sports lesson, spy a victim (more often than
not a rather weak ginger specimen). The victim would be
changing. When his willy became exposed the boys would
descend upon him, grab his willy, pull it and twist it, and
when the victim cried 'mercy' the troupe of boys would
holler a collective triumphant 'willy operation'.

Because of the nature of the exercise, it was only a matter
of years before such activity was frowned upon and scorned
as 'gaywork'. The younger boys or 'juvies' who continued

the practice were looked down upon as being too young to
know better **UK**

windmill, n.

the one old-skool breakdance move that was rumoured to cause testicular gangrene on *World In Action* in 1983, resulting in winding up of school break champion *c.f.* caterpillar

window-licker, n.

derog. term for a spacker. Comes from the 'special' people who ride on 'special' buses sitting on the bus, face leant against the glass, tongue hanging out **UK**

wind up, n.

to tease, for example by telling a false story designed to elicit a particular reaction e.g. telling someone in a block of high rise flats that their lifts were to be disabled to improve levels of fitness in the block's inhabitants **UK**

wind up merchant, n.

a person who habitually teases people by spinning stories designed to elicit a particular response **UK**

wingnut, n.

someone with excessively large or protruding ears (e.g. Prince Charles) *Circa* 1970s+ **UK**

winkle picker, n.

style of shoe popular in the late 1950s and early 1960s that came to a sharp and violent point at the toe. This was supposed to be reminiscent of the type of pin used to extract freshly cooked winkles from their shells. The shoes constricted the toes and no doubt caused immense and lasting damage to young feet. Most popular with teenage boys along with drainpipe trousers *Circa* 1950s–60s **UK**

winnets/whinnets, n.

small pieces of excreta (and other material) that cling to the hair around the buttocks and the buttock cleft of people with less than perfect sanitary habits *c.f.* klingons, dags, arsenuts, cleggs **UK**

wipee, n.
mud smeared down new trousers via the assailant's filthy shoes. Similar to 'Christening'

wiss/wiz/whiz/wazz, n.
urinate, to have a piss. As in 'I'm going for a wazz (etc)' – 'I'm off for a piss'. The term was usually used by boys (naturally) and was in common usage in the playgrounds of South Wales (Swansea) in the 1970s *Circa* 1970s+
UK (S. Wales)

witche's hat, n.
an inverted screwball jammed on a rocket shaped ice-lolly (trade name Zoom) *c.f.* screwball **UK**

woody, n.
(1) an erection, especially when it is clearly visible by pressing against trouser flies.
(2) drilling action administered to the top of the skull with the knuckle whilst the recipient is in a headlock (from Woody Woodpecker) *Circa* 1980s **UK**

woofer, n./v.
flatulence (act or result) – e.g. 'Who woofered?'; 'Did you woofer?' **UK (Mid)**

woot/w00t, exc.
celebratory word. When used online sometimes spelled with zeros in place of O's. i.e. w00t! I just got my licence! *Circa* 1990s **UK**

wotcha/watcha, exc.
greeting used between acquaintances, as in 'Wotcha mate', or 'Watcha cock!' **UK (SE)**

wowser, n.
anyone considered to be trying to stop other people enjoying themselves **AUS**

wrenching, v.
wedgie variation. For example, on someone's birthday reach down the back of their trousers, grab their boxer shorts and rip them off, causing extreme discomfort; hence 'wrenching'. Also you should get a posse of wrenchers together first and hunt down the birthday boy (can't do it to girls cos that's illegal even if it's more fun) and wrench him like a dog! *Circa* 1990s **UK**

wuckless, n.
homosexual

X

xma, n.
misspelling of eczema

x-files, n.
part of phrase repeated interminably by schoolboys once they learn about the solar system. They'd run about the playground shouting 'Here come visitors from Uranus, your anus... geddit... geddit?' and then fall down laughing *Circa* 1990s **UK**

x-men, n.
homosexual i.e. used to be men but now are 'ex' men **UK**

Y

yamp, n.
this was a commonly used term for someone who was from an unimpressive place and who acted like a total twat, and wore very old, cheap and scutty clothes, not unlike a hobo *Circa* 1970s **UK**

yam-yam, n.
derogatory Birmingham term from anyone from the Black Country area *f.* Derived from peculiar dialect e.g. 'y'am away next wick?' (Are you away next week?) **UK (Mid)**

yellow packet, adj.
insult directed at povvos, doleys and so on. Derived from Fine Fare supermarket's economy range of 'Yellow Packet' products. Being seen with a bag of Yellow Packet crisps was tantamount to admitting you were receiving free school meals. 'Ey, them trainers are dead yellow packet they are!' (Used during the early 'Thatcher Years') *Circa* 1980–85 **UK (NW)**

yit, n.
trog, hippy, spod, crusty. Carries implications of being malodorous and socially maladjusted, and quite often Welsh *Circa* 1970s–80s **UK (NW)**

yitney, adj.

cowardly, 'yellow'. Commonly used by teenage boys in the late 1970s when daring each other to perform some kind of competitive task. 'Come on then, you're yitney' would generally provoke a response *Circa* 1970s–80s **UK (NE)**

yocker, n.

spit, gob, flob, expectorate in general e.g. "ee's got yocker on 'is back' *c.f.* spit, gob, flob *Circa* 1970s–80s **UK (NW)**

yomp, v.

'forced' march or run. An 'army' term that came into use in schools after the Falklands War when the public was told 'yomping' was part of paratroopers' training. In schools it was applied to cross-country training *Circa* 1980s **UK**

'you'vegotxma', ph.

ritual cry accompanied by hard slapping on the back and running away rapidly *c.f.* xma

yukker, n.

babies, pre-school age children *c.f.* anklebiters, rugrats
UK (Wal)

'yum yum bubblegum', poem

Classic playground rhyme:

> Yum Yum Bubblegum
> Stick it up your mother's bum.
> Pull her tits, grab some sticks.
> Eat them just like weetabix

Contributor's wife, however, produced the last two lines as she learned them as a child in Wales:

When it's brown, pull it down
Yum Yum Bubblegum

Circa 1970s **UK (Wal)**

yup (ooohh...), n.
disbelief *c.f.* Jimmy Hill etc.

Z

zebbled, v.
lack of foreskin. Term of abuse used in boy's changing rooms as offensive term of address directed towards those in circumcised minority. **UK (NW)**

zinc, n.
not remotely trendy and something to be avoided e.g. If someone had their hair cut and the fringe was extremely straight and short, then that would be a 'zinc' **UK**

zit, n.
pimple, spot, any skin blemish *f.* Geoff Hughes remarks that it's interesting to note that before the 1980s it was unheard of in the UK. However, around that time Jasper Carrott visited America and returned with the word as part of his act. Following a good deal of initial amusement among schoolkids the word has become standard slang in the UK and USA **UK, USA**

zoftig, adj.
pleasantly plump in a womanly sense *f.* via Yiddish from Middle High German *saftec* 'juicy' **UK**

A
COMPENDIUM OF
PLAYGROUND GAMES

a-frame game

this involved a tennis ball and anything over 4 people. It was vital that a corner of the playground tarmac with high fencing was used. This was a very popular alternative to football in Wallingford School, Oxon, UK. The rules are a little hazy, but the general idea was to throw the ball within an uncertain radius and to hit someone with the ball.

Once hit, they had to endure one of two things. They either suffered 'tunnels' – which basically meant everyone (except the poor individual who'd been hit by the ball) standing in a line a foot away from the fence and throwing 'double punches' at the victim, as they ran through the gap in between the line of kids and fence – or they could take the alternative. The 'alternative' was that everyone took pot-shots at the victim – i.e. they threw the ball at the individual concerned while he cowered in fear at the corner of the 'A-frame'... Both could hurt...

This game was very popular with 11-15-year-old boys, and nearly always got out of hand due to the lack of rules. It resulted in bruising, after-school scraps, personal insults, tears and a short-term ban by the headmaster. Obviously it was also an excuse to hit foolish and unpopular individuals... *Circa* 1985 **UK (SE)**

AIDS ball game

frighteningly insensitive version of tag. Whoever had the ball had AIDS and had to hit another person to shift the 'virus' away from themselves *Circa* 1980s **UK**

alley hockey game

budget street hockey, played with any suitable bent stick and a squashed Coke can for a puck

alley-over game

two teams stand on opposite sides of a house. One team

pitches the ball over the roof to the other side of the house shouting 'alley over'. The other team catches the ball and yells 'catch'.

The team with the ball then has the option of returning the ball or doing a 'chase' i.e. running around the house and tagging one of the opposite side with the ball, putting that person out. At the end of the chase the teams exchange sides of the house and all play until a single person is left on the one team *Circa* 1800s–onwards **USA (S)**

bloody knuckles game

a coin, usually a quarter, is spun around. The players try to keep it spinning by flicking it with their fingers. Whoever makes the quarter fall loses, and must put their knuckles on the playing surface, usually a table. Then the winner puts his thumb on the coin, and forcefully pushes it across the table onto the loser's knuckles. The game is played until the loser's knuckles are bleeding *c.f.* slaps *Circa* 1980s **USA**

bobberknocker game

a weight attached to a length of fishing line (making it virtually invisible) operated from a distance so as to knock on someone's window causing them great confusion. For maximum laughs, usually performed on someone of a 'nervous disposition' or someone very old **UK**

bone-head game

an alternative name for the game 'headers and volleys' *c.f.* Headers and Volleys *Circa* 1980s **UK**

british bulldog game

possibly the most legendary playground game. Played on grass. Basically one person tries to rugby tackle one of the other players running from one side of the field to the other. Those caught join the 'catcher', until all are caught except for one hardcase who then has to survive on his own until the bell goes or he gets beaten up for being a smug twat.

Another version was played on a concrete or tarmac surface, but was supposedly declared illegal on school property. However, despite the school deciding to ban playing on tarmac because it was clearly too dangerous for delicate types, some bright spark re-named it Cat's Whiskers and they carried on playing...

Then this version was sent in:

'In our school this was used to describe a game where two teams lined up facing each other, holding hands to form two long lines. The idea was for a person from one team to run over to the other team and break the line by leaping bodily onto the joined hands of two of the players. If the person managed to break their link, their team got a point or something. One of those brilliant games which the entire class played together nicely but the teachers banned 'cos they decided it was too dangerous. Bastards.' **UK**

budding game
the act of throwing buds (from local shrubs) at the windows of innocent householders in order to provoke them into giving chase through the streets of the estate *c.f.* rat-tat-ginger *Circa* 1980s **UK (NW)**

button, button game
played by contributor as a youngster, as in: 'Button, button, here comes mother.'

He writes: 'I remember this as a game for little children. The children would sit in a circle with hands folded (as in a praying posture). The one who was 'it' would hide a button in his folded hands, and go to each of the others, touching fingertips. In the process, he would slip the button to one of the other players. The object of the game was to guess who had the button. The phrase 'Button, button, who's got the button?' came into it somehow, but that's all I recall of the game. If you had the button, you tried to pretend you didn't. If you didn't have the button, you tried to pretend that you did.'

Someone else suggested the following rules:

'The way it was played when I was a kid was that everyone would line up and someone in the line would be passed the button behind their back. Then everyone took off running, and the object was to get to the other side of the field with the button before the 'it' person figured out who you were, and caught you.' *Circa* 1980s **USA, UK**

52 card pickup game
trick usually played by an older child on a younger where, after asking if they want to play, a deck of cards is thrown in the air for the younger child to pick up – while the older runs off laughing *Circa* current **UK, USA (Ohio)**

catch a girl, freak a girl game
played by both sexes usually. Works best with an even number of males and females. Boys are always 'it'. Rules are straightforward. The girls disperse and hide and boys try to find them. When found, the girl tries to escape and while catching her, the boy 'humps' her. After the quick bumpin' & grindin' the girl is taken to the 'pen' where she remains until all the other girls are caught. The game is played with clothes ON **UK**

cats cradle game
complex patterns made out of a loop of string wrapped in

varying configurations around the fingers *c.f.* 'lastics, French Elastic **UK**

chicken scratch game
where someone must prove how hard they are by scratching away at an area of their skin until it bleeds. God knows why! *c.f.* hard *Circa* 1980s **UK (NE)**

chinese football game
played with a football. Players attempt to reduce other player's 'lives' by kicking the ball at the upper-body but without the ball being caught. One kick is allowed per player who may then not touch the ball until another player has done so. There is also a variation of this game in which beatings are administered instead of lives lost

conkers game
conkers are horse chestnut seeds dangling from a string. They are held up by one person whilst another person, similarly equipped, tried to smash their opponent's conker by striking it with their conker. Individual conkers grew in stature with each successful survival of a game... oners... ten-ners...thirty-niners etc. The strength (and thus the life span) of the conker was often enhanced by arcane methods such as soaking in vinegar overnight or baking in an oven
c.f. stamps, stampsies

crazy-daisy game
banned in many schools. All participants link hands into a large chain, the leader starts running around in circles and in a matter of seconds everyone is on the floor bleeding!
UK (Scot)

death square game
(Ed: entered verbatim – I couldn't improve on this)

'A complex, subtle and violent game which emerged in Ysgol Morgan Llwyd school in Wrexham, Wales in the late eighties. It evolved from a game called 'one touch' into 'one touch death square' and eventually, simply 'death square'.

The rules are as follows: a tin can is kicked around within the perimeter of a 20 foot square of grass (we had an ideal one at our school, which inspired the game). Each player aimed to kick the can once, and once only, while forcing another player into a foul. Fouls included touching the can twice, allowing the can to pass between one's legs, or kicking the can out of the square (one could, of course, aim the can to hit someone and then bounce out of the square, for example, thus forcing a foul.) The penalty for a foul was to be subjected to kicks from all and sundry until one had exited the square.

The foul of all fouls, however, was for someone to catch the can in mid-air after one had kicked it. The penalty for this was a 'Chicken Run', where all players would gleefully line up in two parallel rows. The unfortunate offender would have to run between the entire length of the two rows while the other players had a chance to kick the hell out of them.

This was often made doubly difficult by the fact that many onlookers, who had been too scared, or apparently otherwise engaged, would suddenly appear from the furthest reaches of the playground to do their moral duty, thus extending the length of the Chicken Run beyond all reasonableness. A tactic which was sometimes used when taking a Chicken Run was to make a courageous, adrenaline-fuelled leap, attempting to long-jump one's way through the swathe of boots and legs (and, occasionally, fists) in the hope of landing at the far side unscathed. I seldom saw this succeed.' *c.f.* Chicken Run *Circa* 1980s **UK**

decker game
much like British Bulldog but much more violent and prefer-

ably played past a tree with extensive roots *c.f.* British Bulldog *Circa* 2000 **UK (NI)**

double dutch game

(1) variation on skipping rope in which two turners held two ropes flying in opposite directions for one or more jumpers. Rhymes were generally sung and occasionally required the jumpers to perform various tasks as they were jumping, such as touching their toes, turning around, running in or out of the ropes etc. Generally more common in lower-class and inner cities, almost never played by boys. Some minor recognition as a sport in the late 1980s

(2) UK term to describe someone whose spoken or written comments are complete nonsensical gibberish e.g. 'You are talking Double Dutch!' *Circa* 1980s **USA, UK**

down by the river game

this hand game has been popular in the USA for at least a couple of generations. These versions of it were found in Tennessee:

'This was played in a circle. Everyone would stand so that your right hand was on top of someone else's, and your left hand was below the next person's. Every beat of the song you slapped the person's hand on your left. On "BOO" if your hand was slapped, you were out of the circle. If the person missed, and slapped their own hand, however, then THEY were out. When the last two people were in the game, they could have a championship match in the same exact way or they could have a thumb war.

"Down by the riverside the hanky panky
Where the bullfrog jumps from bank to bank you say
A-E-I-O-U Bam, BOO!"

OR

"Ace, ees, Ice, Ous, Oos, Bam, BOO!"
Circa 1930s–current **USA (S)**

duck-duck-goose game

all children sit in a circle. One person walks around the circle, tapping each individual on the head and saying 'duck.' Suddenly, the person taps one person and says 'goose!' and then they run around the circle. The person who received the 'goose' has to jump up and chase after them.

The duck-duck-gooser must run once completely around the circle and sit down in that person's spot before the person they touched catches up and tags them. If they make it, the chaser becomes the duck-duck-gooser – if they're tagged, they're still 'it'
Circa current **AUS, USA, UK**

dungeons game

played at certain North Western schools in Melbourne, Australia where there would be two teams, a boy's team and a girl's team. What would happen was one team would run away, and the other team would try to catch them and then drag them back to the 'dungeon'. Once they were at the dungeon they couldn't run away unless they were tagged by someone who hadn't been caught. Teachers banned the game 'Dungeons', so they changed the name to 'Whiskey' ... and kept playing **AUS**

fainting game n.

short-lived craze for hyperventilation. Came to an abrupt halt when two kids cracked their heads open by fainting and landing painfully on concrete.

forty-forty game

one person would be 'it' and have to count to 40, whilst the others went to hide. The 'it' person would then try to find them, and if they were seen, would run back to base and shout 'Forty forty, I see ****', whilst the others would try to get home without being seen, and shout 'Forty forty home'. The next 'it' person would be the last person back to home, or the first person to get caught. Rhyme accompanying being 'it' was 'No fools around me, above me or below me, no saves alls'. Save all: One person runs back and shouts 'Forty forty save all, and everyone is saved, and the same person has to be 'it' again! *Circa* 1980s **UK (SE)**

french cricket game
everyone stands in a circle with one person standing in the middle holding a cricket bat or tennis racquet. One person has a cricket ball or tennis ball. The idea is to throw the ball at the person in the middle and to try to hit their legs. If they succeed they take their turn in the middle. If the ball misses it is collected by one of the other players who throws it in turn **UK**

french elastic game
similar to 'cat's cradle' where two girls would stand opposite each other with a long loop of elastic around their legs and a third would jump in/out/on it. A vicious tripwire for boys playing fursies *c.f.* cats cradle, 'lastics, fursies **UK**

fursies game
players would try to skim their football card/sticker the furthest, winning their opponents' cards **UK**

ghetto soccer game
informally played in time of extreme boredom, in desert areas where grass is scarce and pavement, dirt and rocks are in the majority. Usually played on blacktop or cement.

Basic play is that a piece of rock, wooden doorstop or generally any other small, hard, non-ball object is kicked back and forth between two or more people, with the object being to either (a) hit the other players in the shins or (b) give it a kick good enough to send it flying into the air, and causing the object to hit something like a car, door or passer-by *Circa* current **USA**

'goat-shagging virgin killers' from the depths of hell game

according to one contributor, this was an 'over-ambitious variant on the tried-and-tested 'Tit'/'Shit' each-person-has-to-shout-it-louder-game. In two years of Physics lessons, nobody managed more than 'goatshgvshhkkkssmmm'. Silly bastards – we should have stuck to 'tit'' *Circa* 1980s **UK**

goomer game

type of football, where someone kicks it to you and you have to volley it into the net. You can't volley without the ball being passed to you by someone else. If you miss the net or it goes over or is saved, then you go in net. If the keeper lets more than 10 in, he gets botty-blasts – you turn him around facing a fence and penalties off all the other players get blasted at his arse *c.f.* botty-blasts **UK (NW)**

green arses

fair-weather game that involves sitting on the grass and having a football hoofed at you. You were only allowed to move using your arms and arse (hence your trousers were then covered in grass stains, giving the name of the game). You were allowed to deflect the ball away with legs only. If the kicker managed to hit you on the back, or above the waist, you were out, suffering the indignity of joining him. The bigger and heavier kids always made easy targets, but reaped revenge with added leg power, kicking the ball at you harder than you could imagine. With arms used for movement, many humorous facial injuries occurred

grog pit game
game of sorts. The idea is that some poor kid is forced into a pit e.g. the bottom of the steps leading to the cellar door, and everyone spits mucus (grogs) at them *c.f.* grog *Circa* 1980s **UK (Scot)**

hacky-pinky game
legendary gladiatorial contest that was banned from every school in Scotland but which was played daily under the guise of its poofy subordinate British Bulldog.

In short, most of the entire school would split into two teams who ranged themselves against each other at the farthest extremities of the playground much in the manner of Zulu warriors. One then waited whilst the decision makers (hardest kids) on the other team chose a victim from your team and called out their name.

In a nightmare-enducing moment the other team would then chant your name over and over again until you made your run, after you had effectively chosen the instruments of your own torture by having to nominate two kids to try and stop you.

Here lay the essential difference between Hacky Pinky and British Bulldog. In the latter, the opponents merely had to 'tig' you to get you out and amalgamated with their team.

In the former, the two basically beat the shit out of you until you went down ... and then amalgamated you with their team. If you did make it across, the whole of your own team rushed across to meet with the opponents who also rushed across culminating in a sort of Armageddon. Scenes ensued reminiscent of the Somme and Passchendaele *c.f.* British Bulldog **UK (Scot)**

hares and hounds game

one team would hide somewhere (usually in our local park) and the other team would try to find them. The object of the game was the first team had to make it back to base without being caught

Circa 1980s **UK (NW)**

headers and volleys game

footy (soccer): A football game with one goalkeeper and the rest outfield. The aim is to score past the 'keeper with either a header or a volley. Pretty simple really *Circa* 1990s **UK (NW)**

hide and seek game

game where one person counts to ten while one or more others hide themselves. On the count of ten, the 'seeker' shouts 'Ready or not I'm coming' and proceeds to meander around until they locate all the 'hiders'. Some rule variations include the seeker to have to race the hider back to a pre-defined spot in order for them to count as 'found' and/or to physically touch the hider for the 'find' to count **UK (NW)**

hikey-dikey game

similar to Knock and Nash but instead of ringing doorbells and running away you attempt to run through all the gardens on a street without being caught. You had to run through the hedges and you got more points the further along the street you got.

It was even more exciting if you played this in back gardens as it was far more difficult to do. In order to get into back gardens you would generally do it by going through your own back garden. This of course meant that if you were caught everyone knew who you were and where you lived *c.f.* hedgehopping *Circa* 1980s **UK**

hopscotch

grid of ten (usu.) squares drawn on the pavement using chalk or a handy stone. Kids hop or step from one square to another in a set routine, avoiding a pebble that has been thrown to mark the square

hot bottle game

played by any number of bored delinquent kids. Quite simply, a milkbottle would be tossed from person to person until it was dropped or smashed and everyone ran off as some miserable old git would lean out of his window and shout at players to 'go down your own end'. The game would often start quite placidly but could be livened up by spinning the bottle as you threw it, rendering it very difficult to catch *Circa* 1980s **UK (Mid)**

kingy/kingey game

name of hugely popular primary school game for 4 played on mini/fun-sized concrete tennis court (sans net) involving using your hand as a paddle with which to pass ball into opponents' area with only one bounce – if the ball bounced more than once you were out; if you paddled the ball outside of the grid you were out. Last child standing *Circa* 1970s **UK**

kingo game

'Kingo' is the name of a game whereby the one who is 'it' initially has a ball (usually a tennis ball) and is not allowed to move whilst in possession of the ball. They must get others 'out' by hitting them on the legs by throwing the ball. The others are allowed to run around in a given area – if they go out of bounds they are 'caught', and there is usually a safe area or 'cree' where they can remain for a limited period (usually a count of 5) to gain immunity from the proceedings.

Those who have been hit on the legs join in with the principal to try and get the remainder 'out', but if anyone who is 'it' is in possession of the ball then no one other than those who have not yet been caught are allowed to move. The rest of the rules (such as whether one who is not 'out' is allowed to interfere with the ball) vary from playground to playground.

This game exists in several versions and has been extant under different names for at least 40 years to the contributor's certain knowledge. It is still played today in South Wales and probably elsewhere *c.f.* cree
UK (Wal)

kerbie game
played by two people standing on the pavement across a (preferably quiet) street by throwing a (cricket, tennis or foot-) ball with the aim of hitting the opposite kerb and causing the ball to return to the thrower. Apparently called Kirkby around the Liverpool area, as Kirkby is an area of Liverpool *Circa* 1970s–90s **UK (NW)**

kiss chase game
game where the boys chased the girls in the hope of grabbing them, and planting a kiss on their cheek. Usually followed by the girls screeching 'eeeuughhh' and wiping their faces

knacker ball game
ball game in which the only two rules were that the teams had to be roughly the same size and that in order to score the team had to put the ball in the opposition's goal. Any means were allowed (including the use of bikes) **EIRE**

knicker-chase game
infants school 'game' where the participants chase the girls and try to pull down their skirts so you could see their knickers. But nobody ever knew WHY.

knifey game
people stand opposite each other. One holds an open knife and has to throw it towards the opponent's legs so that it sticks in the ground. The opponent then has to move his (or her) foot to the position the knife was in, pick up the knife and throw it back in an attempt to make it stick in the ground outside the reach of the opponent. If the knife failed to stick in the ground that turn was forfeited.

The game ended when the opponent simply wasn't able to spread their legs to reach the place the knife was stuck, was unable to reach the knife to take their turn without moving their legs, or (quite often) the knife missed the ground and stuck in the opponent.

In play was much the same as 'split the kipper' but has a more practical title *c.f.* split the kipper *Circa* 1970s **UK**

'knock and nash'/'knock and run'/'knock-down ginger' game
involves ringing random doorbells and running ('nashing') away *c.f.* nicky-knocky-nine-doors **UK (NW)**

knock out wembley/knock out wem game
different name for the game 'Wembley'. Locally, it was standard to have 'every man for himself', rather than teams. Probably because the contributor didn't have all that many players *c.f.* Wembley **UK (NE)**

knuckles game
the same game as Slaps but with a closed fist touching. You would then try to rap your opponent's knuckles with your fist *c.f.* slaps *Circa* 1980s **UK (NE)**

L-shape football game
awkward and pointless ball game invented to make use of irregularly-shaped car parks and bits of waste ground.

'lastics game

played by girls only and involved two people standing opposite one another with a long loop of dressmaker's elastic
around their ankles while a third person performs a complicated series of hops and jumps, chanting appropriate
rhymes. When finished, the height of the elastic is raised to
knees, then thighs, then waist. At this point someone is usually accidentally kicked in the face.

The contributor played this game at school extensively
between 1982 and 1985 *c.f.* French Elastic, cat's cradle
UK (SE)

luggin game

you try to throw a tennis ball from one side of the playground to the other. Simple game but kept all of the boys
happy in the infants. If you could throw the ball all the way
across the playground so it landed on the grass the other side
then you were an 'ace lugga' *Circa* 1990s **UK (Mid)**

maim ball game

(1) an old tennis ball is kicked at a wall (in a manner similar
to squash) while other players stand immediately in front of
the wall and move to avoid being hit at close range.

(2) An alternate is an equally dangerous 'teacher supervised'
game (similar to British Bulldogs) whereby the class has to
run up and down one side of the gym while the PE teacher
launches (with some force) a handsized soccer ball at the
kids. The winner is the last one to be hit. Strangely, this was
considered an end of term treat. The game starts with all
players taking turns to kick the ball at the wall – the ball cannot be stopped and must be kicked from where it ends up. If
a player misses the wall he goes 'on the wall'. Play continues
as before but player on the wall can attempt to prevent a
kicked ball hitting the wall. This is easy if the ball is struck
from afar but risky if attempted at close range. The winner is

the last kicker *c.f.* British Bulldog
UK (SE)

man-hunt game

variation on hide-and-seek where the person has to be physically caught. A variation can be for one person to hide, who then has to be caught by a team of people (whoever else was playing). No distance boundaries were applied – although a time limit was often necessary *Circa* 1985-98 **UK (NW)**

marbles

has many varieties but normally involves the striking of one spherical glass object with another.

There are two main versions. In the first the object is to knock the opponent's marbles out of a ring drawn on the ground (or in the dust) of size determined by custom and practice in a particular area. The object of the second is to hit the opponent's marble three times in succession (or cumulatively – depending on the area). In the first variation, the marbles knocked out of the circle belong to the one whose marble did the knocking. In the second variety the marbles used in the game belong to the first person to strike the other's marble three times.

The game became world famous after Lord and Lady Docker gave it social cache during the 1950s. Individual marbles have been given a number of names depending on their type and quality e.g. these from New Zealand and the UK:

Naked Lady: Similar to a 'cat's eye', but completely clear with no insert. Lead to amusing jokes when held under a running tap about 'Naked lady in the shower'.

Cat's eye: The most common form of glass marble in our games. Clear glass, sometimes tinted, with a cat's eye shaped swirl in the centre.

281

Giant: Oversize marble. Glass versions highly prized, the bigger the better. Plastic versions also appeared occasionally, up to 4cm diameter(!) (which in hindsight looked suspiciously like the ball from a roll-on deodorant bottle). Prized by some (and would probably not have been at the time if we had known where they were from).

Steely: Marble sized steel ball bearing (when) used for playing marbles. Highly prized.

China: A white marble with irregular coloured blobs on its surface.

Spider: Similar to a cat's eye, but with a multistranded tenticular insert.

Bulgarian: corrupted form of ball-bearing. Ball bearings were highly desirable for use as marbles because of their weight and increased surface friction. Using a ball bearing meant your 'strike' was harder – which increased your chances of striking the other marbles out of the circle, whilst itself remaining inside the circle. Knocking a marble out of the circle, whilst you were remained inside, usually meant you got another turn. This continued until either all marbles were knocked out of the circle, or you failed, with one strike, to knock a marble out of the circle. In that case, your marble became one of those available for others to 'win' by knocking out of the circle.

One contributor writes: 'The marbles games I played (1964-68ish, Glasgow) we called "Bools" or "Stanks"; Bools was an open game, one against one, first to hit the other's Bool won. Stanks was a complicated game using the manhole covers on the small drains around the schoolyard in which you had to get your marbles into a certain pattern on the holes that were in the drain covers. A standard marble was a "bool", a large one was a "taw" (worth about three to four bools) and the steelworks in Glasgow meant there were lots of "steelies", ball bearings that increased in worth according to their size.'

Another adds his version: 'On the playground were marked a tennis court and a football pitch. Where the posts for the tennis net would be were holes and the overlapping markings created a rectangular area around it, with the hole being in the centre. Players would take turns to roll their marble towards the hole. Whoever got theirs in first would then immediately be given a chance to roll their opponent's marble. This would then alternate with the winner being whoever got the remaining marble in the hole.

'There were various ridiculous rules and strategies that could be employed (like "cagies", which allowed the non-rolling player to defend the hole with their hand) but ensuring you shouted "nothing in the book except lines" before a match would put a stop to that. ("Lines" meant that if a marble left the designated playing area it would be placed at the point where it left for the next turn, a bit like a football throw-in)

All marbles had values and if you were to play against a better marble, you would have to beat the owner the corresponding amount of times in successive matches.

'The marble hierarchy is as follows:

    Liggy (lowest – and smallest)
    Cat's Eye
    Chink
    Oily
    Steely
    Piratey

'Also, this was a seasonal game, as the tennis posts would appear in the summer. And people rarely played when it rained and dark matter filled the hole.' *c.f.* alley, alley bomper etc. **UK**

mercy game

similar to arm wrestling but carried out (usu.) standing with both hands linked until one party contorts the limbs of the other so much they give a pathetic scream for mercy.

Also defined as 'Two players grasping each other's hands and digging their nails into the other's hand and twisting their arms into positions to get the other person to cry "mercy!" thus ending the game' *c.f.* peanuts *Circa* 1980s

mexican handball game

very similar to A-frame, but played against a flat wall instead of a corner. You throw the ball, someone tries to catch it. If they miss they must run as fast as they can and touch the wall. If someone pelts them with the ball before they get to the wall, the person has to stand (without flinching) as all the other players take a pot-shot at them. If you flinch, everyone gets another shot *c.f.* A-frame *Circa* 1980s **USA**

mob game

variation of hide and seek, where the hiders have to try and touch the 'mobbing post' (lamppost) without getting caught and shouting 'Mob!' *c.f.* blocky, blockie

monkey bar fight game

when two kids would fight whilst hanging from the monkey bars. This was a very popular game at the contributor's school where a league was formed with 'top ten monkey barests'.

The object of the game was to kick your opponent off the bars by any means possible. The most common method was to put your legs on the other's shoulders and kick down. Or there was the contributor's method, which was to kick their wrists and hands *Circa* 1980s **UK**

monkey scrub game

where you grab a school-mate and get him in a headlock, before rubbing your knuckles up and down his skull. Painful. 'I got him and gave him a monkey scrub until his eyes watered.' *Circa* 1984-89 **UK (Mid)**

monkey tails game

takes place with skipping ropes tucked into the waistband of your trousers. Involves person who is deemed to be 'on' trying to step on the 'monkey tails' of fleeing pupils and detach them. Game ends when last monkey is 'tail-less' **UK (Mid)**

murder ball game

(1) played in the Bristol area of UK. Similar to rugby i.e. involved getting a ball into the opposition's goal by any means. This meant that the person with the ball was fair game for any type of attack levelled at him but a man without the ball was safe... in theory. Sometimes played with a medicine ball, which makes it difficult to throw or pass, meaning you have to get the ball across your opponent's line by brute force alone

(2) a game played with a tennis ball, although golf balls were sometimes used when revenge was called for. At the start of the game the players were all lined up in front of a wall. The ball was then thrown against the wall. If you caught or picked up the ball you could throw it against the wall again but you had to remain where you were. If you were hit by the ball, dropped it, threw a ball that hit the ground before it hit the wall or threw a ball over the wall, then you had to stand in front of the wall and were a target for anyone throwing the ball against the wall. If you were 'on the wall' and you caught the ball you got to rejoin the others throwing the ball against the wall. The game was played in whatever time was available to do so. **UK**

'Natalie Nicholson did a poo...' game

Chant sung whilst jumping rope:

> Natalie Nicholson did a poo
> How many dollops did she do?
> 1,2,3,4,5,6,7,8,9' etc...

Presented verbatim:

'Poor Natalie. She was the girl at school that would pull down her knickers on command. Not that we ever wanted to do anything. We just thought it was funny that she pulled her knickers down. The other girls, jealous of the attention she got from the boys, would sing the above rhyme whilst skipping, to taunt her in the playground, as if standing with her knickers round her ankles wasn't humiliation enough.' *Circa* 1980s **UK**

negga game

around fifty pubescent lads played a violent ball game. One lad would start by throwing a tennis ball (but sometimes corky balls had been used by sixth formers) at one of the 50 lads. The lad who had been hit then joined the other lad and they worked together to catch all the remaining lads. At the end of the game you basically had 48 lads trying to throw the ball at 3 lads dashing everywhere trying not to get hit by the ball. The winner was obviously the last man standing.

Negga Tennis was invented, exactly the same game with the odd lad having a tennis racket or bat of some description for added power *Circa* 1994 **UK (NW)**

nervous game

played at most schools. Boy would put his hand up a girl's skirt, starting at the knee, and at every upward creep of his hand he would ask her, 'Nervous?', until she finally shoved him off. Of course, some girls didn't which left most kids feeling a bit silly.

Also a version which starts at the neckline and works down... and in. 'Brave' girls had their breasts 'fondled'... ugly guys had their nuts cracked. Then again, there were those of us who didn't know what to do when the girl didn't react by screaming or fighting you off *Circa* 1980s **UK**

nicky-knocky-nine-doors game
see entry for knock-and-nash. **UK (NE)**

one bounce beats game
group ball game, where the last person who lets the ball touch the floor twice receives a short, brutal round of no-holds-barred beating from opponents.

Sometimes the game consumes the entire population of a playground. The voluntary/involuntary participants cross the whole spectrum of all years. The usual survivors are skilful at kick ups. After a prolonged spell without any violence, the most common tactic used is to shoot the ball against a targeted opponent rendering him powerless to control the ball *Circa* 1980s **UK**

on the hob
one person was 'on the hob' and had to find the rest of the players who had hidden but if one of the hidden players could get back to the hob without being seen then the person who was on the hob, was on the hob again *Circa* 1975+ **UK**

orange balls game
a part of a cruel little game played in the playground. It consisted of a good few kids. All the kids would put their arms around each other until they were in a ring. Then they would chant in a sing-song voice 'Orange Balls. Orange Balls. The

last one to sit down is out' The last one to sit down was then required to go to one side as the rest of the kids would huddle together and think of the nastiest and most insulting thing that they could say about the left out kid. 'X is smelly/thick/ugly' or even more damning 'We hate X'

When decided upon, the kids would then form a circle around the left out kid, and then start chanting the chosen insult at the kid in the middle of the circle. Then the game would start all over again.

Another contributor sends in an alternative definition:
'This is slightly different to the game we played in Bolton, which went like this: Everyone held hands in a circle and skipped around singing twice...

> "orange balls, orange balls,
> woops she goes again"

... then the last person to sit down was the victim, who had to stand in the middle. The other players decided on a person of the opposite sex with whom to taunt the victim, and skipped around them chanting...

> "you love (name of person)" x 4 times.
> clap your hands if you want to kiss him" x 4 times
> "stamp your feet if you want to marry him" x 4 times
> etc.

'... in a truth or dare style. Sometimes they picked someone who you did like, but often it was the kid who always smelled of wee. Then there would always be another player who would grab your hands and clap them together. It took a bit of co-operation to make the victim stamp their feet though.' *Circa* 1960s+
UK

peanuts game

two people stand face to face and interlock the fingers of each hand. They then try to bend or twist the opponent's fingers till the pain is so much he/she has to shout peanuts. If they don't then the game continues. It's great! *c.f.* mercy
UK (SE)

piley-on/1-2-3 pile-on game

always widely announced by shouting 'Pile-On!' which brought everybody running to jump on the pile of legs and arms which would accrue after only seconds. A variant of this wonderful game would involve pointing at large metal, electricity-carrying structures and asking the victim, 'What's that?' with obvious results (pylon). Guaranteed to reduce the weediest kids to tears. Popular on people's birthdays and at the end of term. Often the end result of a 'game' of British Bulldog.

Also defined as 'A term applied when an unfortunate pupil slipped/fell on the playing field during a game of football or British Bulldog'. The cry would draw all boys from all years and all corners of the school to jump on the fallen pupil. The resultant heap could reach up to five feet high, involve up to 30 participants and leave the original kiddie crushed somewhere at the bottom. This ritual is still observed in Wales when someone slips over at the pub. The only difference now is that it is indiscriminate of gender *c.f.* British Bulldog **UK (Wal, Mid)**

prisoner ball game

needlessly violent but much beloved by primary school children until it went the way of Bulldogs and was banned. Played on a netball court, 2 teams would face each other in the end-thirds of the court. A tennis ball (or cricket ball for the really hard people) would be thrown from one end to the other in an attempt to hit a member of the opposing team.

Those hit became prisoners of the other team and stood in the opposition's end of the court, in the semicircle at the end.

They would then try to recapture the ball for their team – if they succeeded in catching it they would run back to their end of the court, as the opposite team used any means possible to stop them escaping. I both loved and hated this. Being a crap shot didn't help, but after the inevitable capture and bruising, I could run like hell to escape beatings from my friends. Too many people got hurt at my primary school, and we were confined to playing rounders – nowhere near as good. **UK**

pussy-in-the-corner game

version of tag or 'chase' played inside playground sheds ('shelter sheds') in Australia. The corners were safe spaces, and players who were not 'he' would call out to switch places from these corners while the one who was 'he' was chasing others. It was considered obligatory to attempt to switch as often as possible. If caught, one then became 'he' *Circa* 1960-70 **AUS**

red-arse game

one student acts as a target by bending over, his 'arse' becoming the target that the remaining students then attempt to turn 'red' by kicking a football or similar in that direction. The redness of the 'arse' remains, as far as I can tell, undetermined as it stays clothed throughout. Contributor says it is a relative of the game he played at school called 'Dancing Dollies' but neglected to send information in on it *Circa* 2000+ **UK (NE)**

red rover game

similar to British Bulldog, but played on tarmac. Two teams face each other in lines across the playground, one member of each team in turn running across and trying to force past the linked hands of the opposing team. Those who are caught join the other team, until only one tough kid is left and has to survive alone or (more often than not) incur the wrath of all the other kids for being so smugly successful *c.f.* British Bulldog, monkey grip

rocky roofs, game

a contributor writes: 'in Australia, when we were kids, and most people had tin/iron roofs, we used to throw a rock on the roof, and run like hell! Used to make a helluva noise, especially on a clear night. It was worse if you were inside the house...a good throw meant the rock would clatter down the roof, until it reached the gutter, or fell over the edge *Circa* 1940s onwards **AUS**

rollerball game

two teams threw a tennis ball to each other attempting to throw it into the opposing goal. Possession of the ball invited a good kicking. **UK (We)**

rugeley

surreal and rather violent game of rugby played often with more than one ball. Involved basically kicking the shit out of everyone and everything. Was usually played on a football pitch to add to the confusion! All we've been told about this is that someone once went down to London and passed through Rugeley station. Further down they would have passed through Rugby station so I can only assume the similarity is from there *Circa* 1980s **UK (NW)**

scavvy queen game

card game. Played more for the mildly painful punishment inflicted on the loser than its riveting gameplay. The 'scavvy queen' was usually the Queen of Clubs. The entire deck was dealt out. You picked a card from your neighbour's hand on each go; if you had a pair, you could put them down. This cycle continued until one person was left with the scavvy queen. They would then cut the cards to determine their punishment. If they drew a black card it was 'hard slaps' i.e. having the back of your knuckles wrapped with the deck of cards, if red it was 'soft' and the cards were instead excruciatingly scraped over the knuckles.

Contributor grew up in Great Yarmouth, Norfolk, UK and played the game regularly and thinks it spread to several schools and other parts of the area too.

For example, this from Gary: 'As well as the aforementioned punishments, diamonds were when you twisted the skin on the back of the hand and spades were scraping the pack, also if you bottled it and pulled your hand away cries of "the whole pack" were elicited and you had to take every card. N.B. this was shouted a lot and was not always fairly applied. Also called Scabby Queen. *Circa* 1980s **UK (SE)**

sea of legs game
played by boys at school using many legs and two tables. The tables were placed side by side, with a gap in between them. Those creating the 'sea of legs' would sit in two rows along the tables, and kick out furiously, thereby creating a dangerous passage between the two tables. Fellow pupils would then attempt to pass between the tables from one end to the other, whilst being kicked hard from both sides. Usually, the lone crusader would fall down about halfway and then be subjected to a good few minutes of severe kicking. Hours of fun, although had a tendency to make people over-excited. **UK (NW)**

sexlord game

half-based on *Doomlord* (a photo comic-strip from the early-80s revamp of the *Eagle* comic, which featured an alien who could 'consume' someone's personality by grabbing their head in both hands), and half-based on ten-year-olds' pre-conceptions of sex.

One person was nominated 'Sexlord' and the rest would scatter. Sexlord would stomp around the playground in a 'slow, but menacing' fashion, arms outstretched, tongue waggling from side-to-side. Sexlord would claim his/her victim by embracing them and making exaggerated noises. This victim would then become a Sexlord and so the game continued until the playground was full of dozens of Sexlords trying to track down the lone survivor.

The game was enjoyed by many for quite some time, until one lad made the mistake of shouting out, 'Last one into the netball court is Sexlord!' at the top of his voice, just as one of the strictest, most easily-offended teachers was walking by. I think just about every class in the school was given a severe telling-off after lunch, but everyone still continued to play the game (thought to have been created at St Joseph's RC in Bishop's Stortford)

There were reports that the game spread to a few other local schools and it was being played at least a year or two after the contributor had left *Circa* 1982 **UK (SE)**

sitting ducks game

harmless game (usually) whereby a number of lower school pupils would gather in a quieter playground and one unfortunate boy was made to stand against an eight-foot wall atop a four foot bank of grass (or mud, if it was raining). The rest of the group would take turns to hurl a tennis ball (often wet and muddy) at him as hard as they could. Moving was allowed, and should the thrower miss, they would join the unfortunate child on the bank. This continued until all but one of the participants was stood on the bank.

Particular pleasure would be gained from causing so much pain to one of the 'sitting ducks' that he fell off the bank, resulting in the playground's most common injury, the grazed knee.

This game was often marred when a sixth former (often a member of the Cricket 1st XI) would pick up a loose tennis ball and would hurl it with all his might at the fattest child. This was a bittersweet moment, as often the fattest child was only tolerated, not actually liked, but the 'them and us' ideal would often result in said sixth former being attacked by a handful of eleven-year-olds. Strangely enough, the same fat kid would often be used as a shield (quite legitimate) to prevent the ball hitting the less principled 'sitting ducks'.
Circa 1990-92 **UK (SE)**

slaps/slapsies game

played at the back of the classroom. Two people put their palms together horizontally, fingertips touching. In turn one person would try to slap their opponents hands before they could move them out of the way. If they missed the opponent would have a go. You could also 'twitch' and try to get your opponent to move their hands before you did. If they did you got a free slap.

Once a person's hands were sufficiently red they were deemed to have lost. Bullies always cheated. Wearing rings was generally not allowed. The more lethal option was Knuckles.

Alternate rules have been sent in:

'Two player game: players hold hands flat in front of each other, one with palms up and the other with palms down. The person with palms up has their hands underneath the other player. This person must take five turns trying to slap the other person's hands before they move them, then they switch.'

And then again there's this offering:

'Thought you might be interested to know that we played the Free Slap rule in Slapsies gaining a free slap if your opponent flinched three times' *c.f.* knuckles, tipsies **UK (NE)**

smiling slut game
simple rules. You smile at the teacher – female preferably – so that she smiles back uncertainly then, still smiling at her, you hiss 'slut' at her through your teeth. Points are scored based upon how confused she looks. Points are lost for being kicked out of class *Circa* 1980s **UK**

soggy biscuit game
probably mythical game in which a group of boys masturbated onto a biscuit, with the last boy to ejaculate having to eat the biscuit. No one has ever admitted to having played soggy biscuit (the homosexual connotations of group masturbation being highly self-evident) yet the legend lives on *Circa* current **UK**

space invaders game
played by sadists. A row of younger kids would line up against a wall, while the shooter would throw a tennis ball or kick a football at them. Each 'hit' would kill off that kid until one smarmy and quick-footed twerp would survive until the bell. (Variety: World Cup – a knockout and progressive football competition, either single player or 2 player teams). **UK**

spazmerrack game
boys-only playground game, and played for one year only! An especially contrived derivation of 'spastic'. The game

would be played with as many people as possible from one's peer group. One unfortunate child would be appointed 'spazmerrack' through the 'ip dip dog shit' selection process. All other protagonists would then scatter across the football field and, when suitably far away from the said individual, would shout 'spazmerrack!'

The spazmerrack would then engage in much flailing of arms and legs, brushing of ears, screaming of non-words and touching of elbows with his tongue in his bottom lip. At the same time he would have to catch members of his peer group who if caught would act in a similar manner.

If the spazmerrack failed to properly demonstrate the stereotyped behaviour expected of him he would be assigned the title of 'hyper-spazmerrack' and would have to lie on his back and perform spazmerrack actions while a new spazmerrack was nominated. Mrs Wright banned the game for its derogatory content and the way children returned home covered in grass stains. *Circa* 1988-89 **UK (NE)**

'spear the queer' game
somewhat akin to rugby, where one lad runs around with a ball while pursued by his classmates who try to tackle him. There are no end-zones, no scoring and any type of ball will do. The entire length and breadth of the playground is the field. Upon being tackled, the 'Queer' throws the ball to the lad of his choosing who then becomes the 'Queer' and must run to evade being tackled for as long as possible. **UK**

spidermonkey game
basically you screamed this and jumped on your friends' or victims' back. They would usually stagger a few more yards or fall to the floor. The 'trick' for the victim is to continue as long as possible as if ignoring the sudden large weight that's landed on your shoulders. How long this went on depended more on the strength of the victim than the size of the spi-

dermonkey! *Circa* 1980s **UK**

spit game

a card game played in school similar to patience with two people; the quickest person to get rid of all their cards wins. So-called because you were supposed to spit when you got rid of all your cards.

Another name for this game was Slam but instead of spitting (I think it got banned) you had to slam your hand down on the top of your pile of cards *Circa* 1980s **UK**

spot game

based on football for numbers from 2 players to however many you can get. Participants take it in turn to kick a ball against a wall. Only one touch was allowed and missing the wall or hitting the ball above a certain height (determined by some kind of mark on the wall) would result in the offender being on 's' – this would continue until a player had collected all letters to make the word 'spot'.

At this point they would have to stand against the wall to become a target for the remaining players. Your reward for hitting one of the boys against the wall was the loss of one of the letters you were on e.g. a boy on 's-p-o' would go back to 's-p'. The game in this guise only seems to be known by people at school in the South of England. Variations were played elsewhere but were known by different names *Circa* 1980s **UK (S)**

spot keeper/spot goalie game

version of Rush Goalie, but with no specifically designated keeper. Anyone who was on 'the spot' at the time, i.e. in a position to save the ball, could act as goalkeeper *c.f.* fly goalie, skeleton goalie, rush goalie **UK**

spuds game

a method used to determine who would be 'it' first. You could have big spuds, or little spuds. Little spuds you just held out two fists, big spuds both hands clasped together. Then whoever was in charge would say the following whilst counting around the extended 'spuds':

One Potato, Two Potato
Three Potato, Four.
Five Potato, Six Potato
Seven Potato, More...
One – bad – spud – means – you – are – not – it.

This would continue until only one person was left *Circa* 1960s–onwards **UK**

stall game

the stallholder would lean valuable football cards or stickers (like teams or club badges) against a wall and the player(s), squatting at a certain distance, would attempt to knock them over by skimming less valuable cards at them. Cards knocked over were kept by the player, missing cards were kept by the stallholder **UK**

stamp out game

kids would tag each other to give or get rid of 'Cooties,' and sometimes the kids would try to tag the tagger right back, so Stamp Out was invented. The kid would shout Stamp Out! and punch his fist into his palm repeatedly. It was also used right before a kid tried to tag you, so the kid with cooties had to be quick! *Circa* 1990s **USA**

stuck in the mud game

combination of tag and simulated oral sex. When tagged, one

must stand still with legs apart, and wait for a member of the opposite sex to crawl between them, thus 'releasing' you from being stuck *c.f.* tag **UK**

tag/tig game
at its simplest involves the person chosen to be 'it' first, running around trying to touch or 'tag' another member of those playing the game. When touched... or tagged... that person becomes 'it' until in their turn they touch another. In most cases the person no longer 'it' can either retire from the game for a rest, or be enlisted by the new 'it' person to help 'tag' the others until there are no more.

The winner is the last one to avoid being 'tagged'. There are an infinite number of variations, some of which are noted elsewhere on these pages e.g. the slightly more violent 'British Bulldog'. Other 'variations' and 'optional rules' are such as these from New Zealand:

Optional rule to alleviate all-out touching/poking/slapping wars between two embroiled parties trying to out-tag each other: Not allowed to tag your master (who is the person who tagged you). This rule means you need at least three people *c.f.* british bulldog, stuck in the mud
AUS, NZ, UK, USA

thax game
involved one child having a ball and other children running around them, in a circle. The ball person would have to close their eyes and throw the ball at the running children. When the ball hit a child, they were out and the last one in was called 'The Thax' *Circa* 1970s **UK**

three and in
game where you had to score three goals past the keeper to then suffer the torment of the other 15 kids hammering the

ball at you. Normally played with a goal painted on a school wall *Circa* 1970s **UK**

thugby game
version of rugby where a soccer ball was used. No scrums, though plenty of rucks, mauls, general mayhem etc. Similar to murder ball *Circa* 1980s **UK (NE)**

tig, tiggy game
equiv of 'it' where one person runs around and 'tigs' the other person who is now 'on'. Variations include 'Tiggy Off Ground' (you're safe if your feet are off the ground) 'Chain Tig': the people who are 'on' have to run around whilst holding hands 'Stuck In The Mud': When 'tigged' you have to stand still legs akimbo unless someone else crawls between your legs without being caught himself.

Another variation on the game of 'tiggy' in Lincolnshire is 'tiggy-off-X' where X is some kind of material. Players were safe while they were touching that material, and vunerable while they were 'off' it (as opposed to the also-popular tiggy-off-ground, where being off ground meant safety).

The best materials were ones with just a few examples well-spaced around the playground: metal and wood were most often chosen. On many occasions people tried to claim safety while touching things on their person, but this was never really allowed – the objects had to be permanent features of the playground, such as benches or drainpipes.

The game usually started spontaneously, with some charismatic child shouting 'tiggy off...' followed by the material of their choice. **UK (Mid)**

tin-can-through-the-legs game
a tin can is kicked and aimed between the legs of opposing players. A successful 'goal' results in beatings administered to the player who was 'scored' through. Known as 'Killer

Can' in the London area. **UK (SE)**

torture/slapsies/knuckles game
a game using the deck of cards to inflict pain and torture on your classmates. One of you holds the deck, the other cuts it. Torture was worked out thus:

> **Clubs**: Scrape (from back to front) the back of the person's knuckles with the full deck.

> **Hearts**: Slap the person's knuckles with the deck

> **Spades:** Stab (back to front) at the person's knuckles, cards angled down (so as to scrape off maximum flesh)

> **Diamonds:** Scrape the cards from side to side across the person's knuckles.

Then the number on the card denoted how many times you got that punishment e.g. Queen of Hearts = 12 x slapping. The loser was the one who wussed out first because their knuckles were bleeding too much *Circa* 1980s **UK**

truth-or-dare game
usually played at slumber parties but sometimes at recess, in which players are given the option of 'truth' or 'dare'. If they choose truth, they must answer any question posed to them (usually something along the lines of 'who do you like'), if they choose dare they must do whatever action someone tells them to.

Rules (from USA):

'The person whose turn it is has the choice of either truth –

where he or she gets asked a question from the other players, dare – where the person is dared to do something without a penalty if refused, double dare – where if refused there is a penalty, or promise to repeat, with a penalty if refused. The penalty if a double dare is refused is usually a very hard two-finger slap on the wrist, which is licked before the slap. The penalty for promise to repeat is first a double dare, and if that is also refused, the double dare penalty comes into effect. You cannot repeat an option or end the game until all the options are chosen by each person at least once, thus everyone experiences the double dare at least once.' **UK, USA**

tunnel of death game
a part of any ball game where some spaz/joey kicked the ball out of the playground into the main road and the rest would line up facing the wall, forming a tunnel with their arms. The afore mentioned spaz/ball loser would then have to journey through the tunnel whilst having the crap kicked out of them.

turnips game
basically, you would go up to someone and ask them what a farmer grows in his fields; eventually when somebody said 'turnips' (or you forced them to say it) you would then proceed to give them a really bad nipple tweak (i.e. turn their nipples around, as if they were the volume control on a stereo, etc) *c.f.* nipple cripple
Circa 1990s **UK**

wall ball game
kids would throw the ball at the wall and then everyone would attempt to catch it as it bounced back. If a person touched the ball but didn't catch it then they had to run to the wall as fast as they could before someone else could get the ball and throw it to the wall.

If the ball hit before the kid got there then they had to stand and face the wall with their ass in the air while the kid who threw the ball to the wall got to throw the ball at them.

A fun trick was to throw the ball very softly at the wall and then, when someone went for it, you would pretend to go for it too but then stop. The person would often look at you and the ball would hit them. Great fun *Circa* 1970s **UK**

walley game

pronounced as 'worly', this is a football game borne of desperation. If there were no coats to make a goal, or one of you was crap in goal, but you had a wall to kick a ball against, you could play walley. A simple rebound game where the ball could only bounce once off the wall before you had to kick it back. The other kid then had to do the same. This usu-

ally went on for hours or until a window went through. **UK (NW)**

wembley game

football based game for teams of 2, generally. Played around 1 goal. Goal scorers leave the field and go through to the next round, until 2 or 3 (number varies) are left. They are knocked out and derided. The qualifiers then get back on the pitch and on it goes – until one team is left *c.f.* World Cup **UK**

'what's the time mr. wolf?' game

chase and catch game. One person would be Mr. Wolf and stand or lean against a wall with his/her back turned to everybody. The others then shout, 'What's the time Mr. Wolf?' Mr. Wolf would shout different times, and each time he did, you had to creep a few steps closer, then eventually he would shout 'Dinner time! Coming to get you!' and run after you in a rather frightening way! **UK (Wales)**

who-wants-to-play

small group of people would decide upon a certain game, but realise that they didn't have a large enough group to play it. Someone would say 'Shall we do Who-wants-to-play?' and we would link arms, and march self-importantly around the playground chanting 'Who-wants-to-play (pause) Brit-ish-Bull-dog?' (or whatever).

The idea was that whoever else wanted to play would link arms with one end of the row and join in the chanting and walking around, until enough players were recruited. Of course, the usual outcome was that you would spend the whole of playtime recruiting players, and have no time for the actual game at all. We would often be rather selective about who we actually wanted to play with us, so would add various disclaimers at the end of the chant – 'Who-wants-to-play... Char-lies Ang-els... on-ly girls... from Mrs Hopkin's class... ov-er six... and no pik-eys...' *Circa* 1980s **UK (SE)**

world cup game

played by teams. One goal, as many teams as you like, and a first-team-to-score-goes-through rule, the last team left being knocked out. The whole procedure would then start again, meaning the first team to go out would wait for ages to get another game.

The great advantage of this game was that it allowed an uneven number of players to stage a fair contest i.e. one in goal, leaving an even number to be split into teams *c.f.* Wembley **UK (Mid)**

x-files game

childish game in which people go into a large closet, turn out the lights and with someone's Torch key-ring, fumble about pretending to be scared *Circa* 1990s **UK**